A Little Bit of HOPE

Father Brian D'Arcy

CAMPUS PUBLISHING

ISBN 1 873223 16 1

First published November 1993

Reprinted December 1993

Acknowledgement

The author and publishers are grateful to the *Sunday World* for permission to reprint these pieces. Sources of quotations are indicated in the text. In some cases it has not been possible to trace original sources: the authors of any such extracts should contact the publishers to ensure acknowledgement in future editions.

Typeset by City Print, Galway
Printed and bound in Ireland by Leinster Leader

Cover photograph courtesy of Bord Failte

Published by
Campus Publishing
26 Tirellan Heights
Galway
Ireland

Contents

Introduction 5

Hope Springs Eternal 7

The Words of Mother Teresa 10

When the Harmless Word Can Cut Like a Knife 14

A Doctor's Dilemma 18

Why Do You Stay in the Church? 21

The Awkward Age for Men — And It's No Joke! 25

The Curse of the Gambler 29

"Saint" Aisling 33

My Brother's Dying Message 36

Jesus: The Facts 39

Suicide: The Inside Story 41

"Love With Heart," Says Kris Kristofferson 45

Would Christ Be Forbidden to Baptise Today? 49

Beware of False Profits 53

Make Love Often 57

Drink: The Devil's Medicine 60

Life After Drugs 64

The Left Hand of God 68

Why I Hated God... And Was Cured By Cancer 72

How To Cope With A Marriage Break-Up 76

A Man Called Peter 81

On The Side of The Angels 84

Women Priests 86

Celebrate You 89

Teenagers, Be Warned 90

The Prodigal Mother 92

The Great Light of Easter 94

Introduction

History is filled with people who held onto hope, who believed that their plans would reach fruition despite the odds.

Alexander Graham Bell was laughed at for his invention of the telephone as "a crank who says he can talk through a wire".

Ludwig van Beethoven composed most of his music during the years of his steadily worsening deafness.

Abraham Lincoln failed in business twice and was defeated in elections nine times. One of the few times he did succeed, however, he became America's 16th President and brought an end to slavery.

Helen Keller, blind and deaf at 19 months, went on to graduate from college with honours and to become a world-renowned author and lecturer who said: "The world is full of suffering. It is also full of overcoming it."

That's what this little book is all about. Human stories. People who seem to be losers, but who keep going. People who struggle with the ordinary things of life, knowing that there is something better somewhere and somehow.

Because they are human stories, you may recognise yourself. Where possible, I've tried to avoid infringing copyright. But I know my ideas are not original. I love sharing what was helpful to me. I hope it will be helpful to you.

I'm not a skilled writer. But I do try to express thoughts as clearly and as humanly as possible. I don't use jargon.

The best way to read this book is to read and article or two and leave it down. Pick it up again whenever the mood hits you.

Pass it onto your friends if you think it might help. And send it to your relations across the water if you so wish.

The hope that I offer is that God is good. That God loves you. That you are lovable. And despite your faults and failings, your life can be a happy one most of the time.

Thank you for taking this book in your hands: thank you for reading this far. I hope you won't be disappointed. Maybe there might be something more than just a *little* bit of hope.

Father Brian D'Arcy **The Graan**
November 1993 **Enniskillen**

Father Brian D'Arcy

Father Brian D'Arcy was born in Enniskillen, Co. Fermanagh in June 1945. He is one of a family of four, two boys and two girls. His father Hugh was a noted Gaelic footballer who played inter-county football for more than a decade.

He entered the Passionist Religious Congregation in 1962. He served for many years as parish priest at Mount Argus in Dublin, before returning to Enniskillen in 1989 as superior at St. Gabriel's Retreat, The Graan.

His career in journalism began in 1967 when he wrote regularly for various pop magazines at home and abroad. He was the first priest in Ireland to be admitted to the National Union of Journalists.

Brian D'Arcy is a well-known broadcaster and television personality. He has his own series of interviews on BBC Ulster and is "Pause For Thought" contributor on Terry Wogan's morning show on BBC Radio 2.

He has broadcast for 2 FM since its first day of broadcast and more recently has his own slot on RTE Radio 1 on "Both Sides Now".

He is a self-confessed "fanatical" sports enthusiast. Gaelic football is his favourite recreation but he's also well-known for his association with Shamrock Rovers and many of the international soccer players are his friends.

Among his more unusual pastimes is his voluntary role as chaplain to the entertainment industry. This brings him in close contact with the major personalities in pop music.

His favourite charity is the Helping Hand Fund, which helps the poor of Ireland, north and south. All proceeds from this book will go to the Helping Hand Fund.

Hope Springs Eternal

Resolutions can be made at any time of the year, because they symbolise the fact that it's okay to make a fresh start. It's giving yourself permission to be human and to have setbacks.

Habits are ways of behaving that are ingrained. They can be good or bad. Habits are different from addictions. We can change habits.

Father Anthony De Mello makes the point:

"Everyone kept telling me to change," he writes.

"I resented them and I agreed with them, and I wanted to change but simply couldn't, no matter how hard I tried.

"What hurt me most was that like others, my best friend kept insisting that I should change. So I felt powerless and trapped.

"Then one day he said to me, don't change, I love you as you are.

"I relaxed. I came alive. And suddenly I changed.

"Now, I know that I couldn't really change until I found someone who would love me whether I changed or not."

Here are a few stories of hope. Stories which will let you know that it is possible to change and that it is possible to do something with an apparently hopeless life.

In my files I have a note about Terry Fox. He once undertook a marathon of hope across Canada.

What made him special was that when he decided to run across Canada he already knew that he had a rare form of bone cancer. Most of one leg had to be amputated. While recovering he got the idea of the marathon.

After months of training he began his run. It lasted from April until September. On the first day his run was given a few lines in the back pages of the Canadian newspapers...but by the time he finished he had inspired millions of people all over the world and helped raise millions of dollars for research.

Although he was dying, Terry Fox found the strength to do something positive. He made his last year on earth meaningful, useful and exciting. He died a hero, even though another man had to finish the race for him.

So what is hope?

Hope looks for the good in people instead of harping on the worst.

Hope discovers what can be done instead of grumbling about what cannot.

Hope lights candles instead of cursing the darkness.

Hope pushes ahead when it might be easy to quit.

Hope opens doors where despair closes them.

Hope carries on despite heartaches.

Hope accepts tragedy with courage.

One lady who accepted tragedy with courage was Marie Bealter. She was once named Wonderwoman of The Year. She deserved better.

She had spent 20 years in various mental institutions because she was diagnosed as psychotic. Her struggle against mental illness was a stunning example of courage and hope.

She had a tormented childhood and was passed from one foster home to another. She was eventually hospitalised for manic depression. Things went from bad to worse.

She persevered and after years and years of therapy and prayer she was released from the institution and was allowed to take on advanced studies. She eventually got a Masters Degree from Harvard University.

What makes the story interesting in the extreme is that Marie Bealter went on to become the Administrator of the mental institution where she was once confined.

That's hope triumphing over adversity.

A better known example may be Betty Hutton. In the forties and fifties she lit up every stage and screen imaginable.

However, she was raised by her mother in an atmosphere of promiscuity and alcohol. It was not the best preparation for a life among Hollywood's fast talkers. And they used her and "tossed her aside like a squeezed lemon."

Naturally her career plummeted. She was unable to cope without the applause. She turned to pills and eventually ended up in a detox hospital. For ten years Betty Hutton struggled through six different institutions. She was sure that she would never ever see happiness again.

Almost miraculously a spark of hope came into her life. It was unexpected too. She was huddled in the corner of a crowded ward when a priest quite near her was being kind to another patient.

On his next visit Betty Hutton decided to talk to him herself. He was a kind man.

Later she said that it was the moral support of the priest that inspired her long journey back to health. Today she lives happily and productively, helping young drug abusers find their way to sanity and health.

In 1946 Catherine de Vinck was pregnant with her second child. She was overcome accidentally by gas leaking from the stove. Her husband saved her just in time. Six months later her son Oliver was born, a beautiful healthy looking baby but there was something wrong.

They discovered that Oliver was blind and severely brain damaged. The gas which the mother had inhaled had reached Oliver, causing a severe, incurable disease. The doctors recommended an institution.

Catherine and her husband Jose decided against it.

However, Oliver was a helpless person all his life. He never spoke or gave evidence of recognising anyone.

Though he was always immobile, on the flat of his back, he never had a bed sore because Catherine and Jose tended him with such care.

He died at the age of 33 and when he did his mother said: "Oliver was always a hopeless case, yet he was such a precious gift for the whole family. He had no apparent usefulness or meaning and the world would reject him as an unproductive burden. But he was a holy innocent child of light. Through Oliver I learned the deepest meaning of compassion."

That's the spirit of hope.

Quoting Scripture

I owe this gem to a Presbyterian colleague.

A Presbyterian minister, visiting his parishioners, knocked again and again on one parishioner's door, assuming someone was at home because he could hear the TV inside.

After 10 minutes he gave up. But before leaving he put his card in the letterbox. On it he wrote "Revelations 3:20". That's the verse of scripture which says: "Behold I stand at the door and knock: if anyone will open, I will come in."

On Sunday a woman handed him her card with the words "Genesis 3:10" on the back. When the minister checked it out he discovered Genesis 3:10 says: "I heard thy voice and was naked, so I hid myself."

The Words of Mother Teresa

Knock has always had a special place in my life. At a time when I was thinking about being a priest, my mother wasn't so sure. But, she thought, a visit to Knock might sort out my vocation.

And so it did.

As regular readers will know, one of my modern heroes is Mother Teresa. She's as close to a living 'saint' as I'm likely to meet.

That's why I was delighted to spend some time with her in Knock recently.

She came into the room looking frightfully small but remarkably fresh-faced. She beamed a smile and sat down. I was speechless in her presence. I don't know what it is but she is so serene, so insignificant and yet she had an awe-inspiring presence.

Her eyes are gentle and clear and apparently all-seeing.

Her hands are worn out from caring. Her feet are too small to balance even her tiny frame properly and her bunions are bigger than her toes.

She looked around. We talked about being honoured by her presence. She simply dismissed any question of honour and she began to talk about holy things and human giving.

She has a habit of raising her hand to fix her veil. You expect a blessing when she does it.

These are some of the thoughts she shared with us.

"Let's do it all for Jesus through Mary," is how she opens every interview.

She has dedicated the European province of Her Missionaries of Charity to Our Lady of Knock.

But it is the poorest of the poor who get her talking.

Mother Teresa: We have taught many people to come to know the poor, to love the poor and to serve the poor. I have seen it not only with our Catholic people, but with Muslims and all religions. The God of the poor has brought joy and peace to many families.

Question: Many people have travelled from the North and from all parts of Ireland today to hear you speak. Do you have a message to say to them today?

Mother Teresa: I have just come from Belfast. Some years ago we were there for a time and please God I hope we can go back there again. My message is to bring prayer back to the homes. Family prayer is necessary. It brings a family together. The family that prays together stays together. It helps us to love one another as God loves each one of us.

Love begins at home. And works of love are always works of peace.

The world has never needed love and peace as much as today. That's why I think we should bring prayer back into the family. That's why prayer to Mary is important. We should pray the rosary in our families. With her and through her we will be able to have a heart full of love. A heart like the heart of Jesus.

Question: Mother, you cherish life and you have given support to people all over the world who cherish life.

Mother Teresa: Yes, God has created life for greater things. To love and to be loved is the most beautiful gift of God. That's why Jesus took human life. He wanted to be one with us. To be with us. To guide us, to love us, to show us the way to become holy. Life is for God only to give and take.

Question: You talk beautifully about what we learn from people who are poor.

Mother Teresa: The poor always accept their suffering and live and die in peace. I have not yet heard any poor person dying distressed or frightened or disturbed or anything.

Especially nowadays. I see our young people suffering with AIDS. We have opened houses for them. They have a most peaceful death. No one has died a disturbed death. I think that prayer has helped them a lot. Peace has come to their hearts, because they have been able to make their peace with God and receive Jesus in their hearts.

Question: Mother, what has your own recent illness taught you about life and death?

Mother Teresa: It has taught me to accept whatever God gives to me, and to be completely at his disposal. Whatever he wants me to do; as He wants me to do it.

Question: Do you have a particular word for young Irish people in a confused world today?

Mother Teresa: Again I say it is very important for them to pray. I have found out that adoration has been the greatest gift of God to our congregation. That's why I believe that if young people were taught to pray and to adore Jesus, many things would change for them. We have adoration in our congregation daily.

In Calcutta we have over 70 young people from all over the world working with us. They are daily at Mass and daily at adoration with us. It's beautiful. They go to holy communion and discover another life completely. They go back home to their own countries happy and content.

So I believe that prayer and adoration in the lives of young people will help them to be really holy.

Question: And what would you say to priests?

Mother Teresa: The Church and the world has never needed holy priests as much as today. It is the same for the priests as the young people. If they deepen their life of prayer, through a deep love and adoration of the Blessed Sacrament, it will make all the difference.

I was with Archbishop Fulton Sheen in New York. He told me that since the day of his ordination, he had never let a day pass without spending at least an hour before the Blessed Sacrament. He believed that gave strength to his work.

I see it in the young people. They are working all day with the dying. Yet every morning at six o'clock they come for Mass and holy communion, those who are Catholic. And then in the evening again Catholics and non-Catholics come for beautiful adoration.

So much more for priests. The most important hour for them, besides the Mass, is the hour of adoration.

We asked Mother Teresa to finish with a little prayer. She cupped her hands, closed her eyes, and smiled so deeply that wrinkles on her face melted. You felt she could see something we couldn't.

This is what she prayed:

Holy Mother of Jesus, you who have a heart so beautiful, so pure so immaculate. So full of love and humility. Help us to receive Jesus in the bread of life, love him as you loved him, serve him in the distressed and in the disguise of the poorest of the poor. God bless you.

She stood up, smiled again, clasping my hands in hers and asked for prayers for her nuns, brothers and priests, active and contemplative, throughout the world.

And she whispered with great delight, that she would soon have her nuns working in China with, of course, the poorest of the poor.

Letting Go

To "let go" does not mean to stop caring: it means I can't do it for someone else. To "let go" is not to enable, but to allow learning from natural consequences.

To "let go" is not to fix, but to be supportive. To "let go" is not to be in the middle arranging all the outcomes, but to allow others to affect their destinies. To "let go" is not to be protective; it's to permit another to face reality.

To "let go" is not to criticise and regulate anybody, but to try to become what I dream I can be.

To "let go" is not to regret the past, but to grow and live for the future.

To "let go" is to fear less and love more.

When The Harmless Word Can Cut Like a Knife

There is no reasonable explanation for our lack of sensitivity when dealing with grief-stricken people. Most of us mean well but end up putting our foot in it.

Which is why this excellent letter from someone who is wrestling with grief right now is so useful. It is not a bitter letter. But it explains the hurt we cause, with clarity and charity.

I am 30 years old. Ten years ago I met a lovely, gentle, sincere man, and four years later we got married, *she began.*

When we first met I was going through some personal problems, and thanks to him I got through them. I never thought that I could have happiness like this in my life.

We both had good jobs and a pleasant future. Soon after we married, my husband's job situation changed and he started up his own business. This meant altered circumstances in our life.

To get the business going entailed a lot of hard work, long hours and self denial. It was a struggle, but it was a joint effort so we worked on. Once or twice things really got bad and I got a part-time job to help us out. My husband really got very depressed in those patches. Despite all this we managed to meet the deadlines and the bills. The business was just starting to pick up a little bit when one Friday morning, my husband, my gentle loving partner, was killed in a traffic accident.

It never made national headlines, but it has altered my life drastically. His life was brutally cut off at 34.

Since his death, life has been hell on earth. Gone was my partner, the love, the hopes, the future. Everything that made life worthwhile.

The business is still going, because I just couldn't make myself sell it or close it down. But the good has gone out of it. We did not get as far as having the family we longed for because we were crippled with bank repayments until the business started to make ends meet.

What now?

A large void in my life, the loneliness, the fear, the sheer hopelessness of it all would drive you insane. People are great when tragedies happen. They can't do enough for you, but soon after that it fades, and sometimes even to the stage of being avoided, because of embarrassment. They drift away and life goes on.

Then it's the endless round of unsolicited advice:

Of course you'll marry again.

Get rid of the business, it will only bring you down.

Time changes things, you'll feel better.

God knows best.

God's ways are strange.

God's will, accept it.

It could have broken a bigger cross.

The list is endless. I just haven't the space to fit them all in.

They can't understand that what's so clean, cut and dried to them, just does not make sense to me at all. I want to shout at God for the unfairness of his death, but I no longer feel God exists. I no longer go to Mass since the funeral, two years ago.

Everywhere you go, so many people are happy doing the simple things of life, and I find the people who give me all the advice on how to count my blessings are those who have never known what tragedy is, and have in their life what is so obviously missing in mine.

I never wanted to be rich, I just wanted a family and a home, and happiness.

Grief is such a personal thing. Everyone's grief is different. Be you six months, six years or 60 years married, your life has been changed by that person. The person you shared your life, your body, your innermost thoughts, your little secrets and worries with, is no longer there.

Nothing seems worth the bother anymore, life is going on for people, but your partner, part of you, is gone. I want so much to believe in God, and heaven, but even that eludes me.

The memories so good, that will be no more, are too painful to recall, the sharing, the little acts of thoughtfulness, cooking special meals, the odd surprises, making love, planning a future, the emptiness of life in the house, the bed, the chats, the silly little worries you would tell no one else, are all gone.

Why are there so many broken and unhappy marriages and my marriage is broken by death?

Why did he die so young?

Why? Why? Why? Why? And no answer.

Time passes. It's later the snide comments come. Some women begin to suspect you. Men are afraid to be seen talking to you.

They remark how well I've coped in the past two years, keeping the business going, etc. What they don't see is that often I go home to my four walls and drink myself into oblivion.

Death would be a welcome relief, but you lack courage even to do that. You get the remarks about not needing money now or money is no obstacle. No money would compensate me for my partner being gone.

Some few will understand, but you don't want to load them with your sorrows. Being with families is too much of a reminder. Your partner is missing, there is an awkwardness about it.

The person who was there to support you in good times and bad, who got you through the minor and major setbacks is no longer there.

Life becomes a prison sentence, which you serve reluctantly.

Bitterness is a big thing, and it can destroy you.

This has taken me hours to put on paper, because it's not an easy thing to do, but it's me and the way I feel. I ask you please to publish it, maybe it might help someone, somewhere who hears the same things or feels as I do. It will help to know that they are not alone in feeling like that.

It might even make someone think before they talk, because there are times when the harmless word can cut like a knife. There are so many questions and no answers.

I ask those who read it, please, please think of those around you in similar circumstances, in your home, work or community. Bear in mind what they are feeling in sadness, loneliness and pain.

Don't shove this God business down their throat. It often drives a person further from Him. Be sensitive, treat them with respect, let them make their own decisions. They did not ask for this tragedy to happen. They are just trying to make some order of what's left.

Treat anything you are told with confidence. Speak about their loved one. Just because it's not in the headlines anymore, does not mean they have forgotten.

Just because they are smiling does not make everything rosy in the garden. It never goes away. Cherish what you have yourself, happiness is the most important thing.

I am sorry for being long-winded, but it's a letter born out of experience. I know people who feel as I do, and feel so lost, because they feel no one understands or cares. What more can I say to you? This is my story and there are thousands of me's.

The Do's and Don't's of Bereavement

Want to show you care when a friend is bereaved, but not sure how?

Do let them know you care — write, telephone or call.

Do be available — to listen, run errands, help with the children.

Do allow them to talk about the loved one they have lost as much and as often as they want to.

Do give special attention to any children in the family — they too are hurt and confused, and their parents may not be able to give them full attention.

Don't imply they should stifle their grief or put a brave face on it; grieving fully is a natural, though sometimes slow, healer.

Don't let your own sense of helplessness or embarrassment keep you from reaching out.

Don't avoid mentioning their loved one's name out of fear of reminding them: *they* won't have forgotten.

Don't point out that they still have other people: people are not interchangeable.

Don't tell them they ought to be over it by now; there isn't a time limit that applies to everyone.

Don't be surprised at mood swings, even after months or years.

A Doctor's Dilemma

There are those who say that every moral dilemma is cut and dried. But life is neither straight nor narrow.

Read this and see if you have a clear, helpful answer. See if you can judge…

I was reading *The Tablet* magazine not so long ago. A Dr. Martin Lupton wrote movingly and heroically about his dilemma as a Catholic doctor caught up in the abortion web in Britain.

A woman was pregnant with an abnormal baby. The baby had a condition known as anencephaly — the baby had no brain.

Being a Catholic, Dr. Lupton could not agree to the abortion and he was arguing his point with another consultant, a compassionate and good woman who favoured abortion.

Honestly, Dr. Martin described the child's condition. He said anencephaly is incompatible with life. With no brain, the baby would not be capable of thought of feeling associated with being human. Babies with the condition, if left to term, can be a major health hazard for the mother.

Dr. Lupton still could not agree with abortion. The other consultant, also a very good person and doctor, thought that such babies should be aborted.

She argued with Dr. Martin: "If it (her word) has no brain, is it human?"

Dr. Martin tried to answer as best he could from his Catholic memory. But he realised that his moral thinking had ended when he was 14, while science in the meantime had leapt forward.

He said the baby was a person from the moment of conception. But he floundered when he came to defining a person. Thought and conscience were essential to being human, he argued.

He mentioned spirit, but his reason kept challenging him to explain how the spirit could be present with no mind.

That's where the argument ended. Both wanting to do what was right, and both with opposite solutions. Dr. Martin said he would not be involved with abortion and there the matter ended. At least that's what he thought.

Being a junior doctor he went off for what would be at best a broken night's sleep.

At two in the morning, the midwife rang for him urgently. The woman was bleeding heavily and looked awful. Could he come at once.

He was angry as he walked along to the ward. Whether he wanted to or not, he was forced into an abortion he disagreed with.

When he got there the woman had already been given two doses of the drug which could make her abort; she was sitting on an inco pad soaked with blood, looked horribly sick and was the colour of death.

When Dr. Martin examined the poor woman, he found sitting in her cervix the body of an 18-week-old foetus. He knew the foetus had to be delivered or the woman would suffer terrible, and unnecessary pain and would bleed continually.

He admits he was scared himself because he had never seen an anencephalic baby.

"Suddenly the foetus became dislodged and being so small, simply fell out of the vagina onto the bed, hitting the side of my leg. I flinched as I felt it. It was dead," Dr. Martin writes.

He describes the baby. Suffice here to say that he remembers the baby had a "squashed up face like a monkey".

The mother asked to see her baby. He placed the foetus on a tissue and gently showed her.

She began to cry. She told him she thought she was going to die. She was a Catholic and thought God was punishing her for having the abortion. She told him she was confused but thought she could do nothing else. She had three other children to care for. She sobbed: "God must hate me, why did He do this to me?"

By now Dr. Martin was in bits too. He felt hopeless. He wanted to tell her that God loved everyone in that room unconditionally, but he knew he wasn't succeeding.

He thought of the extreme pro-life people like Rescue America who present their case with certainty and seem to lack all feeling or understanding. What would they say to that woman?

He thought about the pro-abortion activists. They too make simplistic demands. But they were not the ones sitting in a pool of blood, looking at a dead foetus and crying.

Then the young doctor explained to us where he stands now. Daily he sees Catholic women going for abortions. He believes abortion to be wrong without exception. But he knows too that many of these women are subjected to hypocrisy.

Boyfriends who insist on sex, without any safeguards. Families who terrorise children if they become pregnant. Employers who block pregnant workers. Church people who don't have much time for unmarried mothers.

Why is it only the woman who had the abortion who is blamed? He says that the doctors who, in good faith, provide a service which society mercilessly demands are not to blame either. And he's entitled to that opinion too. (I would disagree, though.)

He made another point which I had never thought of previously. He said that Mary Magdalen was a prostitute and since abortion was widely available at the time, it is entirely possible she had one.

But Jesus didn't dismiss her. Nor did he treat her as more wicked than all the rest. He loved and respected her. And that respect saved her.

"If Jesus had condemned her, all the Church teaches would have been different and I for one would not be a Christian," he wrote.

And then he penned the most sensible and beautiful words of all: "I do not know what Jesus would have done had he been called to Mrs. Smith's room. I do know he would have said to her: 'I love you no matter what, as I love this anencephalic baby and this very confused Roman Catholic doctor'."

That's where we left it. I think that doctor is a credit. Life and death decisions are never simple.

And even if moral principles appear to be clear, putting them into practice can never be as clinical as a theologian's mind.

Don't have a closed mind. Don't judge harshly. Try to understand. Listen to the other person's heartbreak and try to pass on the compassion of Jesus to others.

A little word of advice. If you can forgive yourself, you'll learn to forgive others more easily.

And don't forget a prayer for doctors, nurses, carers and priests who are at the cutting edge. Sometimes we are flattened by other people's dilemmas as well as our own.

Why Do You Stay in The Church?

A couple of Sundays ago, a woman was on the phone to me. She was furious. She'd never enter a church again, she said. She had been severely insulted by a sermon in a Dublin church.

I can infuriate people myself and know the feeling from the other side only too well. So I listened carefully.

I learn a lot from people talking about other priests. I begin to see the mistakes I make myself. I try to make as few as possible. But being human you can't please all the people all the time. And if you say anything worthwhile, it is inevitable that people will feel hurt.

Are you *justified* in feeling hurt, is the real question? Or is it an opportunity to examine your life, because the truth hits hard?

Either way, we priests and ministers are upsetting people more and more by our attitudes.

The woman telephoning complained about the priest's attitude. The gospel talked about keeping the Sabbath day holy. He shouted. He roared. He ranted. He raved. He talked about the people who keep their shops open. He claimed that nobody needed to keep a shop open on Sunday.

He condemned people living together, those who miss Mass now and then, working mothers, separated parents. In short, he vented his anger on a people who wanted healing... and used the gospel to justify his own prejudices... a terrible sacrilege on his part.

He scolded about people who bring children for baptism. He gave out about people wanting big weddings in churches. And the ultimate insult that was perpetrated towards him was when people actually wanted a Christian burial — especially those who might not have been perfect Christians when they were alive!

By the end he seemed to have insulted everybody in the church. Some walked out. Most slept. A few seethed silently.

A couple of other people rang from different places around the country on that same day. It seems as if there was a clerical rush of blood to the head, north and south, east and west.

A man wrote to me from Belfast claiming he would never go back near his Presbyterian church because of what he had heard on that same Sunday.

To round it off, an Anglican in Kent in England wrote a very long letter, only part of which I can use here:

"I have just returned from church. I have never been so offended in my life. Our minister's sermons are usually boring. But today, unfortunately, I heard every word he said," she began.

"He spoke about the desecration of the Sabbath. He spoke about wives going out to work. He condemned everyone who didn't come to his church on Sunday. He personally would never want to marry, bury or have anything to do with those who didn't think it worth their while to come to *his* church on Sunday.

"Those 'living-in-sin' were, to him people who would never see the light of heaven.

"Marriages were breaking down all around, simply because people didn't pray enough. Prayer was the answer to everything. Those who couldn't stick together in marriage were weaklings.

"And finally, he spoke about women not knowing their proper place, either in society or in the church. He complained about the ordination of women in our church and said that he was going to become a Roman Catholic clergyman if his bishop ever ordained a woman.

"What I want to know is: how can churchmen differ so greatly? How can they pretend to be compassionate if they behave as our minister behaved this morning? And is that how you Catholics treat women?"

I'm afraid to answer that one.

Believe me, I haven't even touched the surface of the bitterness which those Sunday sermons left.

If you're a priest and your collection is down, maybe it's because, wittingly or unwittingly, you may have offended more than you thought.

To be honest I was angry myself until I read a recent survey carried out by Father Andrew Greeley in Chicago.

I don't rate Andrew Greeley's novels, but as a sociologist he is top class.

His survey asked the question: "Why do Catholics *stay* in the Catholic Church?"

The bottom line startled him. Catholics stay in the Church because they like to be in touch with the sacraments, especially Mass.

He concluded with some personal reflections. You may or may not agree with them. But don't dismiss him entirely.

1. "The sacraments are of enormous importance to the Church; nothing is in fact more important...

"If politics are too important to be left to politicians and theology too important to be left to theologians, then liturgy is too important to be left to liturgists and religious educators.

"A sacrament should charm the people into wanting more religious education, perhaps, but it ought not to be considered an instrument in the religious education process, much less a means of enforcing conformity."

I hope all those who try to impose rules and regulations with regard to the reception of the sacraments understand precisely what the man is saying.

2. "A sacrament is an encounter with mystery. It is not an occasion for education or indoctrination or manipulation, much less an opportunity for the exercise of clerical power.

"Many religious educators and liturgists, alas, are clumsy, prosaic trespassers in a realm of experiences that are essentially poetic. They tend to be authoritian rule makers in a realm that ought to belong to the freedom of God's Spirit.

"Not quite sure that the Spirit is up to producing the results they want, they try to budget her time for her, thus constraining her to blow the way they will instead of the way she wills. Control of the administration of the sacraments must be wrestled away from such people."

I can see clerical blood pressure shooting up the scale at those statements, and just as the people in the pews blew their fuse listening to your sermons and need to ask themselves was there a grain of truth in what you said, each cleric now needs to ask if there is a grain of truth pumping up our blood pressure too?

3. "Since the sacraments are experiences of encounter with the Holy One, they should be occasions of joy and celebration...

"Thus it is critically important that the sacramental experience be carried out with elegance, charm and not be heavy handed, morose or tedious.

"It is the experience itself — of birth, marriage, reconciliation, renewal — which counts, not the process leading up to it or following after it, (although opportunities for reflection should be made available both before and after a sacrament.)

4. "When one presents oneself for a sacrament one should be greeted with enthusiasm and warmth because one is about to experience great joy. A sacrament is a grace renewal experience and not a reward for having jumped through a series of hoops, fashioned by liturgists or religious educators.

"Nor is it an exchange encounter like the award of a graduation diploma granted after passing a series of tests."

5. "Refusal of a sacrament is not an issue which should normally arise. A Catholic magazine recently carried an article by a religious educator in which he wept crocodile tears about the anguish of having to refuse a sacrament. He clearly revelled in the power that refusal bestowed upon him.

"It's not up to him to refuse a sacrament to anyone. Lay people have a right to the sacraments. Under ordinary circumstances, refusal ought not to be even on the agenda.

"The issue ought to be how to make the experience of sacrament so appealing, so seductive that those who have drifted to the fringes of the Church will be lured back towards the centre.

"This strategy is more difficult and requires more work than laying down the law — which is one of the reasons that it is so rarely pursued."

More Than One Way To Tell The Truth?

A pastor advertised a Church Service for a weekday evening. On the night, the only person to appear for the service was the church sacristan. He was a huge man who weighed almost twenty stone. The following week in the bulletin the sacristan was astonished when he read the report of the service.

It said: "A large and enthusiastic congregation attended."

When he protested to the pastor that the report was a lie, the pastor said: "It is not a lie. You are large and I am enthusiastic."

The Awkward Age For Men — And It's No Joke!

I had a discussion the other night with a group of businessmen about mid-life crisis and male menopause.

The "awkward age for men" always raises a smile. Mind you, it's not a laughing matter for the man or for his family. Doctors will assure you that sometimes the male menopause resembles that in women quite closely. There is a certain difficulty in coming to terms with the fact that life is more than half over. It can have some physical effects as well as emotional ones. Dizzy spells, chest pains, anxiety, headaches, loss of appetite. And that's not the half of it.

It's to do with the rapid deterioration of prospects after the magic 40 has been passed. It's a realisation that if you're over 40, you are no longer young; that today's society revels in youth and beauty.

Look at your papers, your T.V. commercials. Fitness and youth are everything. People are millionaires in their 20's.

A man reaches 45, looks in the mirror, sees a balding head, a sagging tummy, and he realises that in the modern world at least, he's past it.

He starts to go to more funerals than he used to, some of them are friends even his own age. They've died suddenly from heart attacks or accidents. Death is all around.

If you haven't done much with your life up until now, the feeling is worse. It really is a sign of desperation to have reached mid-life and know that your life has been a failure. It's even more devastating to have put every ounce of energy into something which was a waste of time and into a relationship that has floundered.

Some refuse to admit that age is creeping up on them. They wear the latest fashions and are an embarrassment to anybody who sees them. And yet, it doesn't solve the emotional problems.

Somebody in mid-life crisis looks at his promotion prospects and sees that they are probably nil.

He sees his sons growing up, becoming independent. Like a mother whose role in life seems to vanish as soon as the children become self sufficient, so a father sees his son becoming the man of the house.

It often happens that the teenage crisis which many people face occurs at the exact same time as the father and the mother are facing their mid-life crisis. It puts a strain on family life and marriage.

The pretty young girl in the office becomes a challenge.

The wife is a reminder of age, so "let's get away from that" is the common attitude. It's in the 40's that many marriages go wrong.

And the trouble is that very few understand it — which is why you'll find the next quote fascinating.

"All of us have stood at a point where two roads diverged and doubted our wisdom to choose. Many of us have chosen by refusing to risk moving at all; others… have been unaware that they even stood at a crossroads. But some among us have recognised the crossroads and seen in it the path to another beginning."

That's how Gail Sheehy begins her book *Pathfinders* which is a best seller for the past decade in America. No wonder. The book is about what lies deep within each of us — the secret of happiness or "well being" as she calls it.

She spent four years researching the book and questioned 60,000 people in the process. She wanted to find out why some people overcome crisis and others don't. She sought people who not only successfully overcame the predictable crises of life, but who also surmounted life's big crosses — like grief, divorce, being fired, or sickness.

It's fascinating reading.

One of the most interesting chapters is about hunting the secret of happiness. In it she gives ten hallmarks of well-being. They are worth going through, measuring your own reaction along the way. She discovered that really contented people usually say the following ten things about themselves, so, if the cap fits…

1. "My life has meaning and direction."

She found that happy people have a shape and meaning to their life. They find "meaning is an involvement with something beyond themselves; at work, and idea, other people, a social objective." They are people with a goal. They may never achieve it themselves but are happy that they have done their bit so that future generations will have a happy life.

2. "I have been able to handle difficult parts of my life in a creative way."

It's comforting to know that these happy people weren't immune from major upheavals. The happy person was the one who suffered, but who handled the suffering well. An easy life with no major upheaval doesn't bring happiness. It's facing the brokenness of life with courage which matures.

The really unhappy are those who are soured by life, their energy wasted on what might have been. She proved that those who spend their lives "navel gazing" rarely have time to be happy. Get on with life is the best motto.

3. "I rarely feel cheated or disappointed with life."

Most successful people did fail and fail in major parts of their life. The difference was that they put their failure down to experience, learned from it, and turned failure into a successful episode. The pain was temporary and set them on the road to greater things. Unhappy people saw failure as just one more bad hand dealt by life, something which merely fed their own inadequacies.

4. "I have already attained several important long term goals."

Gail Sheehy found that people included things like a comfortable life, family security, and a sense of accomplishment as long term goals. Really happy people, though, would also include family security, love, self respect, and true friendship, as being even more important.

People who blindly followed success were rarely happy.

Those who were least willing to jeopardise family life for professional success were by far the happiest.

5. "I am pleased with my personal growth."

The three most important qualities cherished by happy people were being (a) honest (b) loving (c) responsible.

That's how happy people would describe themselves and would like others to see them. It's obvious that these are three basic Christian values as well.

6. "I'm in love. My partner and I love mutually."

It's an obvious quality of happiness. The author found that "people of high satisfaction not only spent more time than average with the person they love; they want even more time to spend with them."

7. "I have many friends."

Happy people not only found friendship necessary, they found they were able to make friends easily. And they are liked easily themselves. It is a matter of simple expediency. When the chips are down they have more people they can count on for understanding and support. She also found that women make friends more easily than men.

8. "I am a cheerful person."

Being cheerful allows happy people to make friends. The unhappy person was given to severe bouts of depression which in turn made it more difficult for people to become friendly with them.

9. "I am not thin skinned."

Happy people knew their own worth and were not always looking for someone to constantly tell them how great they were. They didn't take criticism of their work as personal. And when criticism came it didn't wash out their sense of self.

10. "I have no major fears."

Happy people were not afraid of time running out on them. She also found that "in every group the most satisfied are also more likely to be religious. A real relationship with God is the first step to happiness."

So there you have it. That's how Gail Sheehy summed up happiness in adulthood.

One little kick in the tail for people like myself was her conclusion that married people as a whole are happier and live longer than those who are single. It applies even more especially to men.

The Curse of the Gambler

There are some problems which seldom get an airing. Gambling is one of them. It's a horrible addiction and here a man who has wrestled with it, shares some of his story.

My name is Bernard, I am a compulsive gambler. It is my privilege to be asked to share a little of my experience, strength and hope. My name is not important, where I am from is not important. What is important is that I say I am a compulsive gambler and I don't gamble today, and that indeed is a miracle.

The fact that I didn't gamble since I came into Gamblers Anonymous is no big deal. I am still as powerless over gambling today as I was then.

What is the big deal about being away from a bet? Am I a better father, better husband, better human being? I let you be the judge.

I gambled compulsively as a child from the age of 12 until I was an adult of 43-years-of-age — always gambling more than I could afford. Gamblers Anonymous is not for people who *need* it, rather it is for people who *want* it. If it was for those of us who need it I would have been in the programme at the age of 12 when gambling cost me more than money.

I became a thief.

I surely needed Gamblers Anonymous when I was married and was unable to visit my wife when she gave birth to our children. I surely needed it when she cried on a Sunday morning with no money in the house. I surely needed it when my children looked for me and I was at the Curragh or in a poker school.

I didn't want it then.

I wanted it on a fine evening at 43 years of age. I lifted the phone, rang Gamblers Anonymous and I knew that all the troubles in my life were related to gambling. All the money troubles, all the family troubles and the job troubles were gambling related.

Somebody once asked me if I had good days in gambling? I certainly had. I won the jackpot at the Curragh one day: I felt 12 feet tall. I have learned, since I found the programme of Gamblers Anonymous, that if I had stayed at home that particular day and taken my wife and baby for a walk in the park it would have been a far greater day, a far happier day.

What did gambling cost me? Sometimes it is said that Gamblers Anonymous is the most expensive club in the world.

It cost me all the money I owned, all the money I earned. It cost me a lot of time, it cost me a lot of sleep.

I fear a telephone ringing, going to work, meeting a postman with a bill again today.

What price? The love I could have given and the love I could have got. I could have taken my child for a walk or to a football match. I could have taught my children to pray or to do their lessons. But as a compulsive gambler these are the prices I pay.

The evening I went to meet my sponsor who was to carry me to Gamblers Anonymous, and I believed at the time to save my life, I was in a lot of trouble. It was during one of our famous bank strikes. I had cheques written with no facilities, and when I met this man he told me I could do with a meeting badly and asked me to come to Limerick, 60 miles away.

I told him I was driving a car but I had no petrol. He had £5 but no car. He bought the petrol and we went.

On the way to Limerick I related the way I felt. I was confused. I didn't know what was going to happen except I knew it was going to be alright. I told him about my house that was up for sale, and my job that was on the line, my children who were afraid.

He told me I wasn't too badly off. He had been where I was, coming out of it one day at a time through the fellowship and programme of Gamblers Anonymous. He pointed out to me that my children were just afraid of me, they didn't hate me, my house was only up for sale, it wasn't yet sold, and my job was on the line but not yet gone. They were wonderful bonuses but he said they were worth nothing if I didn't have the other gift. The desire to stop gambling.

That was the only requirement — a desire to stop.

I learned how to make it easy not to gamble. They say that many meetings make it easy, few make it difficult and no meetings make it impossible. So, I go to a lot of meetings, and I have found it easy not to gamble.

The Twelve Steps

1. We admitted we were powerless over our addiction — that our lives had become unmanageable.
2. Came to believe that a Power greater than ourselves could restore us to sanity.
3. Made a decision to turn our will and our lives over to the care of God as we understood God.
4. Made a searching and fearless moral inventory of ourselves.
5. Admitted to God, to ourselves and to another human being the exact nature of our wrongs.
6. Were entirely ready to have God remove all these defects of character.
7. Humbly asked God to remove our shortcomings.
8. Made a list of all persons we had harmed and became willing to make amends to them all.
9. Made direct amends to such people wherever possible, except when to do so would injure them or others.
10. Continued to take personal inventory and, when we were wrong, promptly admitted it.
11. Sought through prayer and meditation to improve our conscious contact with God as we understood God, praying only for knowledge of God's will for us and the power to carry that out.
12. Having had a spiritual awakening as the result of these steps, we tried to carry this message to other addicted, compulsive people and to practice these principles in all our affairs.

Phone Gamblers Anonymous at:

Dublin 01-872 1133
Cork 021-501501 (8pm - 9.30pm)
Derry 351329
Belfast 249185

I have met my brothers and sisters in the programme who said they loved me because I was a compulsive gambler. My wife loves me, maybe in spite of my being a compulsive gambler. But they loved me because of the disease I carry and because I have the desire to stop.

It is the only way I have ever found in my life to stay away from gambling and be happy. There were times in my life when I didn't gamble because I was broke or I was afraid, but I was very unhappy.

Now, I have a choice. I don't have to go to the dogs, I don't have to play cards, I don't have to go to the race tracks, I am free.

For the first time in my life, at the age of 43, I could see the colour of my childrens' eyes. I could discover their birthdays and their likes and dislikes.

I can today tell my wife I love her without actually saying it: just a smile across a kitchen table, a walk to church on Sunday — what a wonderful life through the fellowship of Gamblers Anonymous.

I believe the 12 steps of recovery are like the 12 rungs of a ladder that we compulsive gamblers climb towards spirituality. There is no religion in Gamblers Anonymous. Spirituality, yes.

I believe a spiritual person is a person who is wanted and needed and loved. There are many people who never gambled who are not spiritual. I believe that in this programme as I do my best I become wanted, needed and loved. What a wonderful way to live.

They tell me in Gamblers Anonymous that I should be grateful. I believe today that all I need to be grateful is to stay away from a bet, one day at a time. I am grateful because I don't gamble and I say thank God.

“Saint” Aisling

Aisling has been in my life for 15 years. She was a young girl, barely into her teens, when she arrived at my doorstep one night, wanting to get married.

Like many of the young people in her area at the time, she was then into sporadic bouts of cider-drinking. And as a result of one of those Friday night binges, she had become pregnant by an older man.

It was obvious to me that a family meeting had been called and that the instant solution arrived at was for Aisling (not her real name) and her friend to marry.

She was young and attractive but quiet and scared. And after a long time talking with them, I persuaded her parents that marriage at that time was not even a possibility, never mind a good idea.

I'm not sure that they agreed with me but they accepted it anyway. Aisling and her boyfriend just lived together when their child was born.

I visited them often because she had very little to live on and anyway she was so disarmingly honest that I always enjoyed talking with her.

She looked after her baby well even though she was barely 16 — and had another on the way.

It became obvious to me even then that she was having a rough time. The bruises were there to see and her boyfriend was seldom in the house.

A second child arrived and this time there was no question of marriage. Aisling, by now, knew that her only aim in life was to get herself and her children to safety and out of the relationship.

In an area ruled by the criminal underworld, it wasn't easy. In a while she did. She walked out of the flat and, I have to say, out of my life, for good. At least that's what I thought.

The years passed. I left the area, and eventually the city, and came north.

And then one day I was visiting a friend of mine who has AIDS. In the hospital corridor I heard a voice calling my name. I looked around and I saw a very sick young woman standing in front of me.

As far as I was concerned I had never seen the lady in my life. But as soon as she told me her first name, the horror of her story struck me. Aisling has AIDS and is often seriously sick as a result.

I sat on the edge of the bed with her and my sadness and my surprise must have been obvious for her to see.

She reminded me of all the incidents so long ago. And she said: "I want to thank you, for not marrying me to that man. I had an awful life with him. He treated me badly. He beat me. We began taking drugs. And then he ended up in jail, leaving me with the two little boys to rear."

When he came out of jail he tried to start the relationship again but Aisling would have none of it. She herself was now heavily into drugs. But even more importantly, she had met another man who treated her with dignity and respect.

With the passage of time though, she lost custody of her two little boys to the man when he got out of jail. It seems that, having taken so much of her life, he was convinced he should take every reason she had to live, as well.

Aisling is not a bitter person, though few have more reason to be bitter.

Since then, the full horror of her story has gradually revealed itself. She became pregnant by her new friend. And a beautiful little girl was born. But Aisling was slow to recover her health.

Just over five years ago, her doctor advised her to go for tests. And they discovered that she was HIV positive. A test was also carried out on her little baby girl. And the little baby girl was positive too. Back then, she hardly knew what AIDS was, but she sure knows now.

Aisling and her little baby have grown closer together. She's made a wonderful job of rearing a beautiful child. She still longs for her two older sons but these days her only interest is in staying alive to be with her little girl. Both of them are often violently sick but both of them remain in wonderfully good humour.

Her family have rallied round and her mother is still as anxious as ever about her "little girl".

Not so long ago I called in to see Aisling in hospital. She had been very sick but was now regaining her strength.

We talked for over an hour about old times and again, she repeated how glad she was that I hadn't married her as a pregnant teenager.

"I would have had a house full of kids and been beaten black and blue every night. Me Ma and myself were talking the other night and we said: 'Wasn't Fr. D'Arcy a great man not to marry us'."

She has asked me to write about her. I think of her often. I talk about her in sermons. I ask people to pray for her. And I honestly think that she's a "saint".

I told her that the other night. And she came out with a few wholesome expletives. She speaks a language that the saints should not know, which convinced me more than ever that her suffering has made her a beautiful person.

Aisling worries a lot about what people think of her as a mother. She worries a lot about what people will think of her having AIDS. She's almost inconsolable that her little girl has AIDS. I think by now she believes me when I tell her she's not to blame. I think by now she believes me when I say we all love her exactly as she is.

Aisling is a part of my, too rapidly passing, life. She was one of many youngsters whom I tried to help.

I always thought that I had failed. I used lie awake at night and listen to them drinking cider and having a party. And I knew that despite their high spirits they were ruining their lives. It was the frustration of it all. And I seethed with anger at those "pushers" who sold them cider.

Aisling, looking back, knows she made mistakes. But she also knows that she has done her best to live with her mistakes. Her body may be racked with sickness, but as a person who risked and grew, and loved and was abused, she's done marvellously well.

She has a few bright things to look forward to in the summer. And I know they are keeping her going these days. She's cared for with great love and affection by many of her friends and family. And nobody deserves it more.

When I spoke with her last she said: "You can call the article 'The Saint'." And she roared laughing again.

She walked me to the hospital door. She planted a lovely kiss on my cheek. And she said, "If anything happens me, I want you to come to my funeral."

My Brother's Dying Message

If you've ever sat beside a dying friend, I know you'll get great comfort from this beautiful letter I got from Australia. It is so well written and so poignant that I pass it on without comment and with a minimum of editing.

This is what the lady wrote:

I'll start by telling you about my brother, Johnny. He was the rogue of the family, always up to some sort of trouble that it would take several volumes to relate. The number of times we fought over his devil-may-care attitude to life and the tears of exasperation I've shed , while trying to sort out one mess after another, don't bear thinking about.

But Johnny was born with a charm that most people can only dream of possessing, and whatever the problems, he could always manage to draw a laugh from me at the end of a stern lecture. A laugh? Sometimes he'd have me in hysterics, and I trying to knock some sense into him.

Johnny had a wife and seven children — four boys and three girls. Each one of them was a precious jewel in his eyes. The youngest is barely four months old.

In dribs and drabs, most of my family trailed off to Australia, myself included, leaving Johnny and another brother and his family in Ireland. We were so busy with our own lives that little thought was spared for the problems we had left behind, except for keeping in touch by occasional letter or phone call.

Then one of those phone calls was to change our lives forever. Johnny rang to say that he had been to the hospital for tests because he hadn't been feeling too well lately and he was awaiting the results. He wasn't one to worry about his health, so the fact that he had actually rung to tell us about this sounded ominous.

He phoned again when the results arrived. Non-Hodgkins Lymphoma — a fancy title that pronounced a death sentence on him. Had it been diagnosed four or five years earlier, the specialists told him, they'd have had a better chance, but they told him that, between them, he and they were going to lick it.

If ever anyone put up a good fight, then Johnny did. From being the black sheep of the family, suddenly he became the family hero. Bout after bout of chemotherapy and radiation treatment took its toll on his body, but he never complained.

His wife has her own memories of his pain and how all his worries were for her and the children. His name is legendary in the hospital where he had his treatment, both for his good humour and his patience.

In November, as the baby was being born, Johnny was rushed back to hospital when his left side became paralysed. A brain tumour was diagnosed, but again the medics assured him that they could shrink it to the size of a pea, and that it would be quite manageable.

However, the lymphoma problem re-activated and he was on the merry-go-round again.

The day before Christmas Eve, a devastating call from our second brother in Ireland came through to Australia to tell us that despite all the optimism of Johnny and the medical team, they were now saying that he had only two days to live.

In spite of knowing that he would be dead when we arrived, my sister and I booked our tickets for St. Stephen's Day. When we arrived, we were relieved to know that he was still there and we rushed straight away to the hospital.

Nothing could have prepared us for what we were about to see. The frail figure with the bald head bore no resemblance to the brother we had last seen, hale and hearty, only a couple of years previously. He was sleeping, heavily sedated as he was with the morphine, and a spaghetti junction of tubes disappeared into a plethora of bottles and bags.

We returned that evening and he awoke when we arrived. He was so happy to see us that tears trickled down his cheeks. We had a little conversation with him, being careful not to overtire him and left early, promising to return early the next morning.

What a transformation! Johnny was sitting up in his bed, remote control for the television in hand, as he flicked through the stations. Although still very weak, he was full of fun and we sighed relief that "our" Johnny hadn't been lost among all the treatments.

And so it continued for two weeks, during which time we said all there was to be said, and more.

He slipped into what seemed like a coma for almost a week and during that time he talked a lot, starting at his own childhood and reminiscing aloud about things he had done, speaking to friends only he could see, and he seemed to progress through time until he was suddenly talking to and about his own children.

He became gradually weaker, with his breathing growing more shallow, until one night we were all gathered around his bed, distraught with tears, awaiting his last breath.

Although Johnny had already received the Last Rites, the hospital chaplain came in to us and said he was going to pray with us, when suddenly Johnny raised his head and said: "Will this be a blessing for the six, Father?" We couldn't believe our eyes or ears! Johnny recited every word of the Lord's Prayer with us. The look of complete love that passed between Johnny and his wife at the end of the prayer would have to be seen to be believed. He drifted off to sleep.

Over the next couple of weeks, except for a few short periods, Johnny spent most of the time sleeping. During one of his alert periods, Johnny sat up in his bed and said: "I want you to get on to all the papers. There is life after death, I know because I've seen it. It's beautiful — and people should be made aware of it so that they can do good before it's too late."

Had this come from anyone but our own "lovable rogue", I think we might have dismissed it as delirium. But for Johnny to be so serious about something like that, it had to have substance.

He died peacefully the next morning. Numb with shock, my sister and brother and I took over the task of organising the funeral. The parish priest had given us a booklet with some readings, asking us to go through it and pick a suitable reading. There was so little time to spare that we were on the way to the Mass when I remembered the reading and I held the book out and said: "Right, Johnny, it's up to you — pick the reading for me."

I shook the book open and the reading, from the Book of the Apocalypse, ran as follows: "I, John, heard a voice from heaven say to me — Write down: Blessed are those who die in the Lord! Blessed indeed, the spirits say; Now they can rest forever after their work, since their good deeds go with them!" We were all stunned that this reading was telling us exactly what Johnny had said on his last day of life.

Meanwhile in Australia, our local parish priest held a requiem Mass for Johnny, with my mother, sister, brother and their families and friends present. When we returned to Australia we were astonished to learn that exactly the same reading had been chosen for that Mass.

Sceptics may say that it was just coincidence but I feel Johnny really wanted to get his message across, and so, Father D'Arcy, I hope you will do what he and John's reading ask and "write down" the message.

Johnny would have been 43 years old today.

Jesus: The Facts

The life of Jesus fascinates us still.

How much do you know about him?

Probably not as much as you think. Here are a few questions and answers. Run through them. A few of the answers will surprise you. Try it out on your friends. You'll surprise them too.

1. When was Jesus born?

We don't know, but most likely around 5 or 6 B.C. which is puzzling, because how could Jesus have been born B.C., which means "before christ"? The reason is that a monk called Dionysus was asked to work out when B.C. and A.D. could be used. His calculations were wrong but the Christians kept that calendar.

2. What language did Jesus speak?

He was born a Jew and the language of the Jews at that time was Aramaic.

3. What did he look like?

We don't know. Again, we presume he looked like most other Jews at the time. There are some who believe that the shroud of Turin was wrapped around the body of Jesus and if it was so, then he was probably bearded and was about 5ft 11ins. tall. But we don't have to believe that the shroud of Turin is authentic.

4. How did he grow up?

Joseph and Mary were poor and Jesus was part of this poor family. They were homeless for a long time. When Jesus was 12 years old, he caused his parents a great deal of worry when he was lost for three days. But between 12 years and 30 years, we know practically nothing about Jesus. We presume that he learned his trade from his father and practised that in the normal way.

5. Was he Mary's only son?

Luke tells us he was "first born" but this term was to used to indicate honour and did not necessarily imply that other children followed him. Reference to his brothers and sisters later in the Gospel can refer to cousins or other relatives. Catholic doctrine about the Virgin Mary is that Jesus was her only son; and this is supported (though not proved) by the crucifixion scene, where Jesus entrusts Mary to his beloved Disciple (John 19-27).

6. What education did Jesus have?

The usual schooling of a working class Jew of that time. Mostly at home, but with some lessons in the synagogue-school, where he learned reading, writing and the stories of the Bible. His own townspeople were amazed at his knowledge, considering how little formal education he had (Mark 6:2). Even from the age of twelve, he knew the Scriptures well enough to argue with the Bible teachers in the temple (Luke 2:46).

7. Did he ever practise his trade?

We presume that he did, because he lived a quiet working life up to the age of about thirty, when he began to preach. Trained in building, he knew the importance of good foundations (Matthew 7:24) and the best location for a house (5:14) and many other practical details of everyday life.

8. What made him change career, as a grown man?

He found his true vocation, when he was baptised by John the Baptist in the River Jordan. Or perhaps we should say, he realised at that moment that it was time to move on to this part of his life's work, to leave Nazareth behind and go out as a preacher and healer to the whole people — first of Israel and then of the world.

9. How reliable are the Gospel stories about Jesus?

Sometimes they are not fully in agreement, nor do they set out to be accurate in every detail. But they convey a true impression of the kind of person he was, the kind of things he did and the quality of his relationship with various people he met. In short, they are a reliable portrait of his personality.

10. Should we take the miracle stories seriously?

Overall, yes. Modern medicine might have different names for the conditions Jesus cured, and might even have treatments which would be effective. But the healing impact of Jesus upon sick and worried people was "wonderful" and that is the basic meaning of miracle.

11. How did he foresee his own death?

Along with the obvious build-up of opposition among his enemies, Jesus had the insight of a prophet to see the meaning of things and how they would turn out. Not only did he predict his violent execution; he even offered it up beforehand, as his ultimate service (Mark 10:45).

12. Was Jesus married?

No. Even though Jewish custom strongly favoured marriage, Jesus chose the celibate (single) life for himself, as more suited to his special ministry. He also called some of his followers to renounce marriage, for the sake of the Kingdom of Heaven (Matt 19:12).

Suicide: The Inside Story

Ever wonder what goes through the mind of a person who commits suicide? Read this.

I'm writing this letter in the hope that you may print it to discourage some person who may be thinking about suicide today.

At 17 my life was at a very low ebb. Things were dreadful at home. I hated coming home as everything I did was wrong in all of their eyes, except my father's, whom I adored.

One night it got so unbearable, I stole a container of capsules and swallowed them three at a time. All the time I thought of my father and God, and asked them both to forgive what I was doing.

I seriously thought I was dying. I prayed to God to release me. I asked him to look after my father. I kept saying to myself: "I'm going to die." This is what you set out to do, now you're succeeding, so why are you afraid?

But I was afraid — very afraid, I kept drifting back to consciousness, thinking, "I'm still alive." How I got through that night I shall never know. When I was conscious, I prayed.

I hadn't the strength to call out for help.

The next morning my father found me. It broke his heart. But he was kind and he really listened to me. The doctor had no sympathy, nor had anybody else. I didn't expect it. I was thoroughly ashamed of myself for what I had done.

The next few days were hell, constant vomiting and black, ugly visions.

Two months later, just as I was getting back to myself, my father died. My whole world fell apart again. I would have thought of suicide again except that the hurt on my father's face kept drifting back to me. I knew if I did it, I would never join him in Heaven.

These days I feel a little better. I realise that with God's help, I got through it. All I can say is that I am glad I didn't succeed. Even so, the physical effects and the emotional scars are with you forever. Let nobody tell you that suicide is an easy way out.

I don't know of any death which causes more sadness than suicide. I don't know any threat which is as effective in upsetting an entire household. It highlights inadequacies. We wonder how we can help somebody who wants to kill themselves. We know that they need help but we don't know how to give it.

And yet, the people who happen to be nearest in a time of crisis are usually in the best position to pick up the warning signs of an impending suicide. They are rarely professionals; they are relatives, friends, neighbours, work colleagues. And each can have a vital role in preventing tragedy.

The best and simplest advice is to be a good listener. Like the letter today, the turning point comes when the potential suicide meets someone who sits, pays attention and listens.

People at risk usually send out some warnings. Some don't, so don't feel guilty if you don't pick up the signs.

The warnings signs may be obvious, such as a change of personality with mood swings. Mood swings are common in young people but if a person is on a down for a long time and speaks of suicide, or if a depression is followed by a sudden high, *be concerned.*

Look out for drastic changes in eating or sleeping habits. Depressed young people may either binge or starve. They may seek escape through sleep or complain of insomnia.

They may withdraw from friends and activities. Everybody needs time alone, but if a normally outgoing friend starts to pull back for weeks, there could be a reason to worry about them.

Watch for people taking unusual risks. It's normal to test your limits. Risk taking is necessary for maturity. But if you see somebody doing things that may seriously endanger themselves or others, find out why.

Abuse of drugs or alcohol: it's always a dangerous sign when people have to turn to artificial means to feel good.

They start making final arrangements. People who think they won't be living much longer tend to tie up loose ends by giving away treasured possessions, or making peace with family and friends.

If you see a friend not performing at work or at school, as well as they used to, or if they begin to grow obviously untidy and don't care about their appearance, then that could be a sign they need help.

In short, look out for a workmate who seems particularly anxious, the elderly person who is unwell and living alone. The bereaved relative, the friend who has uncharacteristically been caught shoplifting, the vulnerable adolescent who had been jilted. They may all be at risk.

Teenagers may be particularly vulnerable at times of crisis or change.

People who are used to succeeding but are suddenly faced with failure are also at risk. They can be high powered businessmen, or brilliant students.

How can you help? You need patience and understanding. Don't be over anxious and above all, don't rush in with solutions to their problems.

There is nothing more aggravating than know-alls who smash you up with paperback psychology. They give out facile answers and they don't even have enough compassion to try to understand the problem. They are a menace.

You may need to allow people to talk about suicide. The betting is that they will be too ashamed to speak about suicidal feelings. They can often talk about marriage problems, housing, sexual problems, money. But they need to be able to talk about the taboo, the death wish, without feeling guilty. Talking about suicide doesn't put it into somebody's head. On the contrary, it reduces the risk.

You can listen. It is probably the single most effective way of helping somebody who is suicidal. You may not have another opportunity and you can never underestimate the healing effect of somebody who listens without judging.

You can let them know that you try to understand how awful they feel. You can encourage them to cry.

You can accept their frustrations. Sometimes when they are accepting their frustrations they begin to explore options. The realisation that there are options may be the most healing thing of all.

Allow them to feel bad.

Little phrases like — "When everything comes at once it gets on top of you", or "You must feel at the end of your tether" are lovely phrases to hear.

Try and get them to see somebody who is a very good friend. Almost everybody has what the psychologists calls "a significant other" in their lives.

Often suicidal thoughts come when that "significant other" has abused friendship or maybe deserted the friend at a moment of stress. You need to be aware that such a crisis may be the cause of suicidal thoughts.

A promise to keep in touch is a help.

If someone tells you that they intend to kill themselves, ask them how they intend to die. You will not make things worse and the knowledge may be crucial to save their lives later.

Tell them about the Samaritans. Every area has a Samaritan number. Make sure they know it.

And two final little pieces of advice.

The first is to know your limits. You cannot make choices for others. You cannot live their lives for them or keep them alive if they are determined to die. But maybe you can keep them alive long enough to get help.

And lastly, the best way to prepare yourself for helping a suicidal risk is to recall some of the worst times in your own life. How did you feel? Who helped you? How did you get over it?

What Is A Grandmother?

A grandmother is a lady who has no children of her own, so she likes other people's little girls best.

A grandpa is a man grandma. He goes for walks with boys and talks about fishing and stuff.

Grandmas don't have anything to do except to be there. Grandmas drive you to the supermarket where the pretend horse is and they have losts of coins ready. Or if they take you for walks, they slow down past pretty leaves and caterpillars.

Grandmas never say "Hurry Up!"

Sometimes grandmas are fat, but not too fat to tie kids' shoes. Grandmas wear glasses and funny underwear. They can take their teeth and gums out.

They answer questions like "Why do dogs hate cats?" and "How come God isn't married?"

When they read to us they don't mind if it's the same story again. Everybody should try to have a grandma, especially if you don't have a TV, because grandmas are the only grown-ups who have got time.

Composed by a girl aged seven

“Love With Heart,” Says Kris Kristofferson

I’ve written about Kris Kristofferson and his songs so often that I fear the accusation of self-indulgence.

I love the man, always have since I first discovered him about 22 years ago. When “lonely’s more than just a state a of mind” I listen to his songs and find he puts words on feelings I didn’t know I had.

I met him and daughter Tracy three times on his visit here. I’ve seen his shows a dozen times.

There are those who think of him as an actor — and he did have success in *Convoy* and *A Star is Born* and *Heaven’s Gate*, to name but a few.

Regrettably, his stand in defence of the underprivileged in Nicaragua and South America has meant that he’s not asked to make films anymore.

It’s a strange turn of events for a man who was steeped in an army background. His father was a Pan Am pilot who went into the Air Force during World War II which meant that Kris was brought up near a base in Brownsville, Texas.

Dad became a Major General and was in charge of the airlift operations during the Korean War.

But Brownsville itself had a bigger influence. He was looked after by a Mexican lady who was as close to him as a mother. He spoke Spanish before he spoke English. She gave him insights into how the poor live and think.

After he graduated from college in America, he got a Rhodes scholarship to Merton College, Oxford. He immersed himself in Literature.

“For the first time in Oxford I got in touch with some wonderful, mindblowing people like Shakespeare and William Blake. It was a great experience for me. But I went from there into the army, carrying all of this inside me and I'm lucky I'm alive today. I did everything I could to be self destructive.

" I spent three years in Germany and volunteered for Vietnam — I was absolutely suicidal."

By then he had a daughter and wife. That same daughter is staring at him in disbelief as we speak. It seems as if this is the first time she had heard it.

But Tracy is a special daughter to Kris.

Tracy is in fact the "kid" in a classic Kristofferson song "Jody And The Kid". It tells the story of the break-up of his first marriage. He used to take Tracy around the bars while he wrote and traded songs. His wife didn't see much future in it. Before the break-up Kris took Tracy around the bars to say goodbye to the old hard-drinking friends, who had grown to love her.

"One old hard-hearted man saw us come in and said into his beer: 'Look yonder comes Krissie and the Kid'. I couldn't write it like that so I changed my name to 'Jody'. That was the first good commercial song I wrote," he says.

Last time I spoke to Kristofferson in an extended interview was when he appeared at the RDS years ago. On that night he was distracted.

"Yes, I remember it well. I was on tour then with the late Roy Orbison and Jerry Lee Lewis. The night before in London they talked to me about the children. Both of them had children who were tragically killed in a fire and in a traffic accident.

"I had just got word that Tracy had been the passenger on a motor bike which was in a horrible smash. She was by now seriously ill in California. Orbison and Lewis agreed on one thing. They said that if you ever lose faith in God, you should ask for the impossible and stand back.

"The night I spoke with you, was the next night in Dublin. After the show I was told Tracy would not live and if she did, she could be brain-damaged. I could take no more. I pulled out of the tour and flew back to LA. It was the longest plane trip I have ever taken. And when I got to the hospital, I nearly lost my mind.

"Tracy was on life support. There were tubes everywhere. I thought they were waiting for me to arrive before she died. I thought of what Jerry Lee and Roy Orbison said and all I could do was ask God for the impossible and stand back.

"Just then the doctor came in. He looked at me and his face lit up. He said: 'I've just seen her foot move'. Tracy continued to recover. And that is the very same precious daughter who is sitting right over there."

At this point she seems shocked to hear the story of her life and Kristofferson himself dissolves in tears.

He insists he is not a religious man in a conventional sense. But he is equally adamant that he is a Christian with a personal faith in Jesus.

Ironically his biggest hit as a singer was "Why Me Lord?" (He also co-wrote "One Day At A Time".) One journalist tried to imply that he wrote "Why Me Lord?" as a send up of Gospel music. To suggest that to Kristofferson, one would need to stand well back these days. It still makes him angry. For Kristofferson it was a genuine expression of his deepest faith.

There's a story in every song. Legend has it that the late Roger Miller got "Me and Bobby Magee" from Kristofferson when the latter was a janitor in the record studio.

It's close but not quite accurate. Miller was the biggest country star in the world then. He came into Nashville and Kristofferson volunteered to work the weekend as a clean-up man just to get close to this legend.

"I was working in Columbia studios and Miller just rolled in. He was all over the place. Those were the days when Miller was a living testament to better living by chemicals. He rattled. He was climbing the walls.

"He pulled out a suitcase and pretended to talk into a phone. He didn't record a thing. He was high.

"Years later he remembered me and invited me to Los Angeles to write new songs for him. In fact we spent all day every day by the pool and not a song was written.

"We were on the plane back home and Roger said to me: 'I hear you have a good song. Let's hear it'. I taught him "Me and Bobby Magee" on the plane journey to Nashville. We went into the studio and recorded it when we arrived and that was the start of big stars recording my material. I owe a lot to the late Roger Miller. Super character."

Janis Joplin also had a million seller with the song.

I've often suggested that Kristofferson wrote his material when he himself was feeling at his lowest. He expresses his lowest moments best.

He wouldn't totally agree.

"My bad times are other's good times. But I hope that even in my songs which describe the lonely side of life, you'll see hope. There is passion but there is also resurrection. All my songs have a spiritual element. The people who understand my songs are in spiritual communion with me. Otherwise there is no point to it."

It's probably why he spends so much time speaking on behalf of the poor and those suffering injustice. He had many priest friends who led the option for the poor movement in South America. And he is savage in his condemnation of the Catholic Church's hierarchy in South America who align with right wing oppressors.

On stage he speaks out against American imperialism. For him the Third World War is already on. It's the fight to give the poor a just share of the good things of this earth.

"Freedom is a wonderful thing as long as it's free for everyone," he says.

"William Blake made it an obligation to be true to your creative spirit. He said if you bury your creative talent in the earth, even if you want natural bread, sorrow and desperation will pursue you through life to death and after death, shame and confusion, to eternity."

I asked him to sum up his thoughts on life in a sentence and expected a line from the haunting song "To Beat The Devil" — where he beats the devil of despair by drinking his beer and stealing his song. Instead he thought for a moment and said in a low pained voice:

"Tell the truth;
sing with passion;
work with laughter;
love with heart."

Would Christ Be Forbidden to Baptise Today?

An astute parish priest who ran a good parish decided to go on a golfing holiday. But being a good parish priest he had already made sure that his curate of two years was well trained. That is to say, he did what he was told! And would always ask before taking any initiative. He was, in clerical parlance, "a very safe pair of priestly hands".

On the morning of the golfing holiday, an important parishioner died. (Defined here as from a respectable family — one which gave no trouble). But the parish priest had no doubts about going. There was a safe pair of hands in charge.

On his return, he checked things with the curate. A detailed report of all events was given.

"And how did the funeral go?" asked the parish priest.

"It went quite well, I suppose," answered the curate with great respect and in a low, flat, voice, the way holy young lads are supposed to speak.

"The only wee *problem* was the Church of Ireland choirmistress, Mrs. Armstrong came up to Communion."

"And what did you do?" asked a slightly breathless, though well-tanned parish priest.

"Well, she was in my line and I didn't see her until she was two people away. So I just did what I thought Christ would do in the circumstances," answered the curate in an ever more masculine voice.

"Ah, good God," screamed the parish priest, "you didn't do a thing like that!"

I first used that story 20 years ago giving a talk to priests in the west of Ireland.

Strangely, only priests laugh at it. Most lay people think that's exactly what we clergy would say.

Like all good stories, if it's not true, it could be. And that's the bit which isn't funny.

Churches, like other institutions, have been sidelined into irrelevancy. Much of it is their own fault.

The *second* most sensible statement I heard from a bishop recently (read on for the most sensible) was when Bishop John McCarthy of Austin, Texas, told his priests to get down off their high horses and stop putting impossible impediments in the way of those people who came to the Church for sacraments, especially marriage and baptism.

Good. More sensible talk like that and people might actually listen again.

He said he was alarmed at the frequency with which people were turned away from the rectory because they couldn't measure up to parish policies or diocesan guide-lines. No wonder nobody listens.

"It's time priests realised their primary task is to help people find Christ, not turn them away," he said.

"Many couples are made feel unwelcome, and are devastated when they are met with canon law and stupid regulations, such as, "You are outside our parish, we don't know you long enough"."We don't see you at church, so we can't allow your child to be baptised", etc.

Worse still is the attitude: "Unless you do our programme, we are not letting you have marriage/baptism."

What arrogance!

"It's time these priests realised that programmes are helpful, but they are at best guide-lines. It's time priests with real pastoral enthusiasm were allowed to get on with their God-given task," the good bishop was quoted as saying.

He also said we shouldn't impose middle class niceties on the poor. Well done, Bishop!

Wouldn't it be marvellous to hear such a welcoming, encouraging word from someone locally?

I often think that if Christ came to work in today's churches, he would be forbidden to baptise, conduct a wedding, and probably banned from preaching as well. No wonder we have made ourselves irrelevant.

But then dwindling dictatorships always strike at their own hearts, attempting to hold onto power.

That's one side of the church.

Another is summed up in the *best* statement I've seen from a bishop recently — namely the Irish Bishops' Statement on Unemployment.

Just because the churches, in some areas make themselves irrelevant, we shouldn't dismiss everything.

With unemployment reaching 350,000 radical steps must be taken.

Unemployment is a divisive issue, make no mistake. That's the tragedy.

Recent governments have tried, as hard as they are allowed, to do something about unemployment.

They have failed, but at least they tried.

What is needed is a concerted effort. Those with money and power will have to share it. Those with talent will have to work together. It cannot be a question of employees and employers holding on to what they've got, looking for more and to hell with those who have nothing.

It is not a question of parties sniping from the side-lines. Nor is it a matter of unions versus employers. Neither has much of a future unless work is created.

All organs of society, those with power in the media, in politics, in the marketplace, and in churches will have to settle their differences and work so that those marginalized, suffering, hopeless human beings and devastated families find some solace, some hope.

When the boss's son and the union leader's daughter and the media mogul's brother and the bishop's niece can't find a job, or when they lose their house, then we'll have action.

When the T.D.'s family have to emigrate and spend some nights on the streets of London, then we'll get the ideas and the money and resources coming together.

It's funny how we all accept a level of poverty in other people's families but we'd scream in anger about it in our own.

And it's amazing when money speculators manipulated the markets unacceptably, how hundreds of millions can be found to protect the monied people hurt by them, right across Europe.

There is no money to help the poor. But there are billions to protect the rich.

When the budget comes, there will be an outcry if there is an attempt to raise company taxes, personal tax or freeze pay. Banks and building societies are already in there, lobbying where it hurts.

But unless those who *have*, do with less, there will be nothing more for those who *have not*. So why the pretence?

Everyone has a right to life, adequate food, a basic education, reasonable health care, and a decent home.

No one has a right to an excess of the good life, overladen tables in sinfully wasteful restaurants, endless education, luxurious suites and elaborate machinery in hospitals, and a choice of several homes in various continents , no matter how hard they've worked.

We have no right to condemn people to miserable poverty-stricken lives. The resources are there and can be found to bolster banks and fight useless wars.

So why can't we have the money, the ideas and the energy to fight poverty and lessen the unemployment crisis?

Tell me, because it beats me.

Smiling in Church

The following is an excerpt from a letter sent by a parishioner to her parish priest.

In Church last Sunday I was intent on a small child who was turning around, smiling at everyone. He wasn't gurgling, spitting, humming, tearing the hymn books or rummaging through his mother's handbag. He was just smiling.

Suddenly his mother jerked him around, and in a stage whisper that everyone could hear, said: "Stop grinning! You're in church!" With that she gave him a belt on his backside and, as the tears rolled down his cheeks, she added: "That's better," and returned to her prayers.

What must they think, these children of ours? We sing, we make a joyful noise unto the Lord, but our faces reflect the sadness of a Charlie Brown at his pessimistic worst.

Suddenly, I was angry. It occurred to me that the entire world is in tears. I wanted to hold this child with the tear-stained face and tell him about God, the God who had to have a sense of humour to have created the likes of us.

I wanted to tell him that he's an understanding God — one who understands when little children are bored in church. What a fool, I thought, this mother sitting next to the only life left in our civilisation, our only hope, our only miracle, our only promise of infinity.

If he couldn't smile in church, where was there left to go?

Beware of False Profits

Some of the revelations about business deals in this country have been so horrifying that they cry out for instant condemnation.

On the other hand, they're so horrifying that perhaps they condemn themselves.

What I've got to say is not directed at any particular company or any particular scandal or any particular set of revelations. I merely use the most recent selection as an example of something that I've said many times.

Namely, there are many ways to rob people. You can do it with a gun, you can hit them over the head, you can break into their home, you can snatch their handbag, you can steal from their shop.

Or you can, in a designer suit and chauffeur driven Mercedes, do it in style and be glorified by a gullible society.

No matter how hygienically it is done, there is only one word for it. Robbery. Nothing more, nothing less. Whether it's corporate robbery, whether it's immoral dealings within the rules of finance or whether it's pointing a gun and snatching the takings, it is still robbery.

The more I talk to successful businessmen and women the more I discover this fact. Many of them try their best to abide by the rules set down in business ethics. Almost all of them consider it fair and right to keep the rules which govern finance.

The problem is that the rules set down for the ethics of business dealings may have absolutely nothing to do with the rules set down by the Ten Commandments or natural justice. They have absolutely nothing to do with social obligations. And that's the crux of the matter. They live in two different worlds.

Men and women in high places consider it perfectly fair and just to abide by the rules of their institution, even though it drives a coach and four through every rule of decency and basic morality.

Let me lay it on the line: Thou Shalt Not Steal applies to everybody. Whether you're in a designer suit, a Mercedes, your private plane, Roman collar, pushing a bike or joy-riding in stolen cars.

A society which fails on that basic principle is bound to collapse.

We've watched, with a certain satisfaction, the collapse of the communist empires throughout the world. Capitalism, if it continues to be abused in the way it is in these countries, will also cause its own collapse.

Nor am I Government bashing. That is a red herring. The people I hear government bashing now, themselves played that very same game when they were in office not so long age. So their new found conversion cuts no ice with me.

The bottom line is that, no matter how much time a minister spends on the job, if the rules of the game are wrong he's not likely to get the right result. And it's the rules of the game which are wrong. They need changing. It would fit us all better, moralists and politicians if we set about trying to achieve justice. the rules of the game have got to change before justice will come.

You might as well blame a referee for a bad game of football. He can apply the rules but, if the people playing the game don't want to play football, no referee will make them play football. No minister can insist that everyone in a state company acts honestly. Even less so can he insist that everyone in a private company acts justly.

It is a crying shame that with so much poverty in the country, with massive unemployment, and with a major recession staring us in the face, all we can argue about is who's to blame for paper money flying between various companies.

Can we get *real money* so that people can get employment? Can we get a share of that money which will help to put bread on people's tables? Can we get a share of that money to improve necessities of life like education and health?

The only way we can get real money is by changing the rules of the game so that exorbitant profits and overly powerful billionaires cannot bleed us to death. That's the kind of justice I'm looking for.

Remember: Thou Shalt Not Steal.

We know the conventional platitudes which say it's a dog-eat-dog world out there; you've got to do it to them before they do it to you; the golden rule is those who have the gold make the rules; don't make waves; you've got to go along to get along; keep your eyes open and your mouth shut; charity is fine but business is business; buy low, sell high.

You hear what they say about the poor: they are scum. They deserve what happens to them. They made their own destiny. We work hard for what we've got. Nobody's doing us any favours so why should we do them any?

That is not an unfair summary of the ways of the "successful" business world. Can I just bring you back to what St. Mark's Gospel, Chapter 10, says about that: "Those who seem to exercise authority lord it over them. The great ones make their importance felt. It cannot be like that with you. Whoever wants to rank first among you must serve the needs of all."

The revolution that Christ is calling for is far more radical than any political revolution ever launched. It's far more radical than the thundering editorials, or some of the I-am-not-as-the-rest-of-men, rantings and ravings of some politicians.

Justice means firstly giving every person what is due to them. If we give away in charity something that we have acquired unjustly, then we are giving away something that is not ours to give. Before giving in charity we must first give to others what is due in justice to them.

And I'll make a further point. We have to give back what is not ours before we can give away what is ours.

Thou Shalt Not Steal refers to work, business, commercial dealings, profession and style of life. *Thou Shalt Not Steal* is about paying a just and fair wage for a job and about doing a just and honest job for that wage.

Thou Shalt Not Steal covers buying and selling, it covers employment and redundancy. It covers contracts and promises and delivering on time.

Thou Shalt Not Steal talks about fair prices and just profits. Not to put a tooth in it, *Thou Shalt Not Steal* tells us to beware of false profits.

Thou Shalt Not Steal binds the chairman of the company and the cleaner in the office. That's the bit that rubs. It's all right for us who haven't got to sit back and snipe at those we think have got. It's easy for us to be loud in our condemnation of what we regard as immoral on their part.

But I have to be honest in my dealings. I have to do an honest day's work for an honest day's pay. I've no right to steal in the office. I've no right to claim dole and work. I've no right to take days off claiming I'm sick if I'm not really sick. Neither have I any right to overcharge if I own a shop. I've no right to sell inferior goods, turn out bad workmanship, draw money for work that is not done.

I've no right to live beyond my means while not meeting my bills.

Being cute and clever and beating the system is almost always stealing. It is not "Business Drive" getting ahead.

It is not "getting round" the law. There is no way to get around the law of God. *Thou Shalt Not Steal* has no exceptions.

Whether you're the chairperson or the charperson your actions have consequences. Repeated acts of dishonesty by one person can amount to a grave injustice. Injustice has a chain reaction. It means that businesses are wrecked. Factories are closed. People's right to earn a living is ruined.

This can be caused by unjust management or it can be caused by unjust customers. How many jobs have been lost because people would not pay and because management neglected their business? Both are equally damaging.

Each has said: I wasn't the only one to cheat. As if that was any justification. You stole and you will have to suffer the consequences on the day of judgement.

Nobody has an absolute right to anything. Nobody can say I can do what I like with my money, my profits, my property or my land. There is no absolute right to any of them. We have a right to private ownership but it must always have a social function.

"There is no U-Haul after the hearse. There are no pockets in the shroud. You cannot take it with you."

That should be a reminder of how we should use money and wealth. When we get to the Pearly Gates, money will no of no earthly use and will certainly be of no heavenly use.

Make Love Often

It must have been Saint Valentine's Day which prompted it.

I was with a middle-aged married couple who had been watching a television programme on *The Joys Of Sex.* I missed the programme. But I was there for the follow up.

The married couple posed a simple question to me. "When was the last time you preached a sermon encouraging married people to make love often?"

A simple question. To which you might guess there was a very simple answer. "Never."

Admittedly, I have frequently advocated frequent love-making in marriage.

The couple said that adverts, films, television programmes, magazine articles and novels all show sex as friendly, warm, attractive and enticing. They all make positive statements about sex — it's good, it's desirable, it's wonderful, it's a necessary part of committed life.

On the other hand, religious groups, especially the Catholic Church, they say, seem to put so many restrictions on sex that the lasting message is *Sex Is Bad.*

I was losing the battle but I did point out that if you search through any church document on sex, it will tell you that sex is good. You'll find plenty of positive statements about sex in church documents.

They countered that words on pages mean nothing. To begin with, only priests read that stuff anyway. And even among priests, the percentage who read it is deplorably small.

Furthermore, even if lay people did read it, the language used is so outdated and technical that it would put you off sex for life. It doesn't ring true!

Is there more to religious teaching on sex than The Brides of Christ?

The husband made a valid point when he said that the church has given up on sex. They have simply lost the battle. The world is saturated with superficial images of sex. The church sits on the sidelines and repeats the boring formulas.

If you ask the average person what the church has to say about sex they will tell you that everytime a Roman collar comes on the television to talk about sex, you're left with the impression that it's dangerous, sinful, not nice and to be avoided at all costs. Some of the worst are Protestant ministers — who practise a little sex themselves, one hopes…

The Church is anti-abortion, anti-sex before marriage, anti-contraception and therefore seems to be anti-sex. The only time sex is good is when it's for making babies.

I thought he was a bit harsh saying that. But it's very hard to argue against it.

Sex is seen as a kind of a necessary evil — providing you don't take pleasure in it. That could be said to be what we *actually* preach, even though it's not what we *intend* to preach.

I was reeling. So the wife came in with a sucker punch.

"We all know what you're against, but can you tell us what you're for?" she asked.

I refused to answer. In fact, I was getting hot under the collar. Even we clerics experience hot flushes at inappropriate times and inappropriate places.

As usual, in situations like that, I came out with all guns blazing.

I'm for sex.

Human sex is good.

It is not dangerous.

How could it be? It was God's idea in the first place.

Loving pleasurable sexual intercourse is wonderful.

It is not a sin. In fact, shared sexual pleasure in marriage is a sacrament, a source of God's grace and probably the most complete prayer that a married couple can make.

So there!

And I went further. I said it's much easier for us priests to talk about sex than it is for many lay people. I could guarantee that if I advertised a lecture for any day of the week, under the title "Sex and Pleasure in Marriage", about three people would turn up and they'd be nuns!

In fact, the only priest who is famous for talking about sex is Andrew Greely. He's also very wealthy. But those who take the trouble to read Greely's novels will discover that in most cases he's simply saying that sex is good. Yet, the normal person thinks that Greely is way out and maybe not a real priest at all.

Not true. He's a very orthodox priest.

I had scored a few points but there was more from the opposing corner.

"The only time we hear a sermon about sex is when you want to condemn it. You warn teenagers about the dangers. You go to great lengths telling us that we shouldn't get AIDS. And you go to equally great lengths to tell us we shouldn't wear condoms which might actually prevent those foolish enough to mess around, from getting AIDS."

In truth then, sex is a problem.

A teenage son was listening in. I was expecting him to run out of the house mortified. He didn't.

He said: "Everybody knows that sexual intercourse inside marriage is on the decrease."

I didn't ask him his source but it had a ring of truth about it. The boy could be right.

"So, why doesn't the church have a campaign to promote more sex within marriage?" he added.

The next thing they'll be suggesting is that priests display car stickers proclaiming: "God loves the good love-maker." Or it could be "Make time to make love".

The mother shifted position.

"The bishops have had pastoral letters on everything. If they believe sex in marriage is good, couldn't they have a letter promoting sex in marriage. They could tell us to be creative."

(I think she intended the pun).

"They could tell us that the more often we make real love in marriage, the closer we come to God. Sex isn't just a natural inclination, it's a supernatural inclination. Sexual attraction is a grace from God."

The last word came from the husband, as it usually does.

"We're glad you came in tonight, Father. We wanted to tell somebody in the church that Catholics have a lot of good news about sex and it's time they told the world. Surely the church is not embarrassed by sex, are they?"

I didn't answer the question. I didn't even finish the cup of tea. I had nothing more to say.

So, I left, defeated.

But the more I thought about it, the more I realised that the couple were right.

Drink: The Devil's Medicine

A few weeks ago, a Limerick student wrote to me expressing, very well, the fears he had about his mother's drinking. She terrorised himself and the family, as well as half the neighbourhood, by drinking and driving.

It brought an expected avalanche of post.

Drunks ruin families. Drink also kills. Occasionally, it kills the drinker, but more often it kills some innocent person.

A man from Dublin wrote to me, explaining how he feels. He is a recovering alcoholic in his mid thirties. When you read his story you'll see that he has every right to offer advice to the Limerick student. He was quick to recognise that there was strong alcoholic type behaviour in the way the mother drank.

The writer says: "I don't think I can stress enough that denial is the most disturbing attitude of any alcoholic. It is the only reason why your mum is behaving as she does. She is denying her drinking and she is denying that she has a problem.

"I can understand how concerned you are with regard to her drinking and driving. I too wish for her sake she would be caught and put off the road before harm comes, either to herself or others."

And when you read the next paragraph you'll see why the writer is anxious that she should be put off the road.

"I can only speak from experience and having to live with remorse for the rest of my life with what I did as a result of drinking and driving. I killed a person.

"It took a fatal accident with the loss of a life to make me finally realise and admit defeat over alcohol.

"I will never ever have peace of mind again, having deprived a family of a loved one. I often sit and wonder why it was somebody else's life and not mine that was taken. I would much rather have died myself than to live through the hell that I'm going through now.

"I have just been put off the road for life. It is a small price to pay. But God, I would hate to see your mum going through what I am going through.

"Try and get her to a couple of AA meetings or better still get her introduced to an AA member. She may not require hospital treatment and nowadays there is nothing to be embarrassed about. It is a widely accepted disease like any other and, while there may not be a cure, there is a solution. The solution is not to take that first drink.

"Presently, I am living day to day, I have overcome drink. But I can never overcome my conscience."

The article prompted reaction from far afield. A regular reader in the Bronx in New York wrote:

"Your recent article, *Why Does Mother Drink?* prompted me to write.

"As I was reading the article I was full sure that it was a brother of mine who was writing the letter. The young Limerick student's feelings could have been the feelings that any of my family had a few years ago.

"My mother, as did many other mums as I realise now, drank herself drunk and out of control for many years. I was the oldest in our family and took over most of her duties, like housework, meals, laundry etc.

"When my youngest sister was born, mum was forced into getting help for herself. She was admitted to hospital. It took three hospitalisations and a lot of help from AA before she quit for good...hopefully.

"My heart went out to the young student, I often felt like that person myself. Sometimes I felt worst. I wanted my mother to die so that an end would be put to all the fights, the upsets, the tears, the anger, the frustration, the embarrassment.

"I thoroughly agree with your advice. You have to get on with your own life. Your advice to the young person was absolutely perfect.

"I had a super dad who spoke openly to all of us about mum. He also had a great sense of humour and as he often said, he was an incurable optimist.

"Just knowing that you're not the only one in the world going through this helps, more than somebody who has never gone through it can possibly understand.

"The young Limerick student shouldn't be ashamed of his mother's problem. If he takes your advice he'll learn that there are many others in his position and only too willing to help him.

"He doesn't have to envy other families either. I know at times this happens. But as you grow older you realise a lot of people have a lot of hidden problems. If it isn't alcoholism it's something else.

"My mother's alcoholism, believe it or not, brought all of our family close together. And every day I thank God for the open, understanding and loving father He gave us.

"I know that this isn't always the case. From experience I realise that the children of alcoholics have to overcome the attitudes of both parents. Because the spouse of the alcoholic can go through life denying the problem or avoiding it in some other ways.

"I wish you could tell the student that there is life after his type of childhood. Thankfully, I'm happily married and enjoy and appreciate my parents very much now."

That was the kind of advice which was echoed in almost every letter. Dozens of children of alcoholics wrote in, saying that once you seek help the problem becomes manageable.

A person from Co. Down had a slight variation of attitude.

"This is the first time I've ever written a letter to a paper," she began.

"The dinner is only on and I know it will be late. But I don't care as my family are always well looked after. I felt that I wanted to write to you and what I have to say is more important than anything else at the moment.

"Please tell the young Limerick student that he is brave and thoughtful and kind. My heart goes out to him. I too have someone close to me an alcoholic. My husband, whom I still love very much, is an alcoholic. But after many years I simply took a stand on my own. I went back to night school, went to art classes and got on with my life.

"I have four lovely children. They all love their father very much.

"I have talked with them, cried with them and encouraged them — all as a result of their father's drinking. But I have shown them that one's life need not be destroyed by a person with a drink problem.

"As much as you love that person, we all must stop trying to control his or her life and get on with our own. It's hard to do but it works and it's the only thing that works.

"The young student should come to understand that if he gets on with his life it will help his mother to come to terms with her drinking. She herself will have to face up to the fact that she is an alcoholic. Probably, within her own heart, she is already facing up to it but hasn't the courage, just yet, to cope with it in the open."

Finally, "Alan" asked me to look at his thoughts on the subject of drink abuse and crime. He knows what he is talking about. Read this.

"I am 23 and in prison. The first time I was caught I was only nine years old. Even then I remember that I was an experienced robber. I was robbing long before I experienced either drinking or smoking.

"At nine I robbed a Ford escort. I had driven less than two hundred yards when the police car drove up behind me.

"I panicked and drove straight into a wall.

"I can still remember the cop who nicked me. He had big feet and spoke with a culchie accent.

"He said he was taking me to a station which we all knew was like a Gestapo headquarters. At the time I didn't know what Gestapo meant, but I knew this particular station sent a cold shiver of fear down my spine.

"At the end of the day I got bail. My mother put up the bail.

"After I was arrested, I was the local hero amongst the 'gurriers gang'. I was the first one of the gang ever to be arrested and I had actually seen the inside of Gestapo headquarters.

"I never wanted to see the inside of a station again, but I now had to live up to a reputation. I had to act the hero. I was scared. And the only way I could live up to the thieving image was to get drunk.

"As a result, I spent most of my teenage years in and out of jail. I was never hit or hurt by my family. Sometimes I think it might have helped. But then again I saw others who were beaten by their families and it was a deterrent for a while, but not for long. We had long bragging sessions about who got the worst hiding.

"For me the daily doses of hour long lectures were worse than a hiding. By the time I was 13 and 14 I was a hardened drinker. And when I was drunk I would rob anything. And I'd do anything for a dare. I was into "smash and grab" and "jumpovers" in a big way. I did it only when I was on drink. I could earn more money in an hour than the cop who arrested me could earn in a month.

"I began to take LSD when I was 15. That was the year I was sent to St. Patrick's prison for stealing a car when I was drunk. I got three months. Over the next years I was in and out of jail constantly. I was drinking, taking drugs and robbing and getting caught easier because I was drunk.

"I took LSD for five years. I have snorted heroin only once but sniffed gas and petrol regularly. I took my mother's valium and once injected cocaine.

"The pattern was that I robbed when drunk but wasn't able to rob when I took drugs. I needed to rob continually to feed the drug habit.

"Many of the people locked in prison are there because of drink related crimes, yet there is very little rehabilitation in prison. I am convinced that it is drink — the devil's medicine — which has caused my life of crime."

Life After Drugs!

Drugs are a big problem still. Too many people have died. Too many are on the way.

That's a fact.

There is another fact which is not so obvious. People can overcome addiction. Many people do. Two people share their lives here. And what they say is encouraging. They have felt the powerlessness of addiction. They have experienced the joy of a new drug-free life.

Read and see.

"Dear Brian,

"I began to take drugs at the age of thirteen. At the time I felt isolated and somehow different from my friends. Drugs seemed to be the answer. They offered me an escape. I quite enjoyed it initially, mainly smoking hash. I felt part of something and it gave me an identity.

"As my drug-taking increased it began to affect my schoolwork. I had to steal and engage in various criminal activities to get money. I couldn't stop. I was in constant trouble at home, at school and with the police. By the time I was seventeen I was injecting heroin on a daily basis.

"I managed to get a good job and moved to the country where I thought there would be no drugs. I immediately started drinking. I started abusing prescription drugs which I obtained from doctors. I tried to cut down and to stop but it just got worst. Although I always worked I got into heavy debt and invariably reverted to crime.

"Coming back to the city I started injecting heroin again. I spent between £500 and £1,000 per week on drugs. I lived in constant fear of the police. I also had to worry about the people I mixed with. We would have robbed each other at a moment's notice.

"My life was full of fear, anger, loneliness and isolation. I had lost all my friends and family. I also lost any self-respect or dignity I ever had. I couldn't bear to look at myself in the mirror.

"Eventually I was arrested again. My probation officer suggested I attend an N.A. meeting. I went reluctantly. I *did* want to stop but didn't believe there was life after drugs.

"I met people there just like myself. There were people from all walks of life who had problems with all manner of drugs. I learned about the disease of addiction. I discovered that will-power alone wasn't enough.

"I kept going to meetings. The fact that there were no leaders or rules attracted me. It is just a group of men and women, for whom drugs had become a problem, helping each other lead drug-free lives.

"That was several years ago, and I have been clean ever since. I have a happy and productive life today. I now have a successful career and friends. I am a better person.

"That's it. I wanted to let people know there is life after drugs. I have been given back my freedom and now have a choice. This has been possible as a result of the help I received in Narcotics Anonymous.

The second letter comes from a wife and mother who uses the name Bernadette. She too has been saved by Narcotics Anonymous.

"I feel compelled to put pen to paper and to write about the effect that drugs and alcohol had on my life. I was an active alcoholic and drug abuser for 15 years. I began when I was 14 years of age. I used prescription drugs mostly from doctors, hospitals and chemists. And vodka was my god.

"I found that taking drugs and drink blotted out my reality. I was in a permanent haze. I could never cope with what was going on with me — my memories of my childhood — my parents were both 'extremely dysfunctional' people, to use a cliché.

"Drugs — valium, napps, codeine, anything I could get at the time — kept me going. Alcohol was still the greatest thrill of all. I used prescription drugs on a daily basis. I never saw them in the same light as hard drugs. Now I do see them in the same light.

"It is not what drugs we used, it is the way we used them, to take away our reality and the feelings and memories we couldn't cope with. Drugs for me were just something that I needed. I had to have them at all costs. I would have sold my soul for them.

"I married when I was eighteen and a half years of age. By the time I was 26 I had four children. During the years my children were growing up I never got to know them. All I could see was that the more money I spent on my family the less I had to spend on drink and drugs.

"My family were always in my way. I never had enough money to feed my addiction. I always had to lie and manipulate people for money, even though I knew in doing so I lost all honesty and self-respect.

"Active addiction is a truly downhill spiral. During the last four or five years of my addiction, the nightmare I was living got worse and worse.

"I resented my children and everyone around me.

"I couldn't see that drugs and drink were causing massive problems within my own family. My children hated me in the house and were always asking me to go out. It got to the stage where my eldest daughter (then nine years old) would be telling me to wear make-up, I looked so bad.

"All through my active addiction I blamed everyone and everything for my life. I was resentful and envious of those who seemed to have their lives together.

"It was only towards the end that I could see I had a problem — a massive one at that. I spent my time justifying my need for drugs and drink. I thought that because I was in an average home, and my kids never missed school, that I hadn't a problem, despite the financial mess I was in.

"I didn't know what the words honesty, responsibility, love, care, feelings, self-esteem, self-respect (and a whole lot more normal human emotions) meant.

"Today I am nearly five years clean, thanks to the 12-Step Programme of Narcotics Anonymous. I have been to hell and back. I ended up in a psychiatric unit for a detox for two weeks, which was absolutely dreadful. The withdrawals and *delirium tremens* ("the DTs") seemed to go on forever.

"When I left the hospital I made a commitment to myself to see what it would be like to live without drugs and drink, to stay alcohol and drug-free.

"I go regularly to N.A. meetings. There, for the first time ever, I've got understanding and support. In the beginning I went to the meetings on a daily basis because it actually nurtured the desire to stop using drugs and alcohol, to change my life and become a better person.

"Today I love my husband and children, who have given me fantastic support. I know so much about my children. I truly love them and care for them. Today I am a loving, honest and responsible person.

"I've seen miracles happen in N.A. — people who come in just like me, without a hope in the world, spiritually and emotionally bankrupt, and who — like me — healed themselves through the power of one person helping another in the fellowship of Narcotics Anonymous."

Both writers mentioned Narcotics Anonymous. N.A. is a non-profit society of men and women for whom drugs have become a major problem.

They are recovering addicts who meet regularly to help each other stay clean. You don't have to be "clean" when you go to N.A., but after the first meeting, they suggest that you keep coming and stay clean.

You don't have to wait for an overdose or jail sentence to get help from N.A. Those who come are told that they are not hopeless cases. It is possible to overcome drugs with their help, especially the Twelve Steps programme.

Addiction is a disease which can happen to anyone. You can become hooked on drugs because you enjoyed them, or to suppress feelings, or because of medication for another ailment. Others became addicts because they joined the crowd once and found they couldn't stop.

Addiction is a progressive disease, like diabetes. Addicts are allergic to drugs. If life has become unmanageable through drugs, and if you want to live without drugs, The Twelve Steps will be basis for a new life.

The "Twelve Steps" for recovery from drug addiction are as those for recovery from addiction to gambling.

Read them in "The Curse of the Gambler" on page 31,

The Left Hand of God

Why should I look at a beautiful woman and enjoy it? Who is the whore of Babylon? How come the young are the only people of faith today? Read on and find the answers.

Richard Rohr is not a German soccer player. In fact, he's a highly articulate American Franciscan priest. He has a cult following in this country.

Because of him, I am sad today. He has had an operation for cancer. I hope it will be a successful operation. We can only hope and pray.

Richard Rohr lives on the edge. He founded a community called the Jerusalem Community. It is comprised totally of lay people. The authorities didn't like it, mainly because they had no control over it. But it was very successful. And when he established it he moved on to another task.

When America went to war in the Gulf, Richard Rohr was one of the few sane voices who stood for peace. Perhaps the suffering he endured gave him perspective.

If you're disillusioned with your church and you feel that the institutions as we know them, are huge crushing, power-hungry ones, then read on.

This is a loose paraphrase of his thoughts. In simple language, this is where I'm at today. If religion means anything, this is it.

Rohr points out that many New Age people confuse introspection with spirituality. They think that if they gaze at their belly button long enough, they are somehow becoming more holy.

He says that spirituality is about letting go of the false much more than it is collecting the new, the therapeutic or the helpful.

If I had my way, I'd nail that notice on the door of everyone engaged in the formation of priests and religious today.

"To be spiritual really is to look at what's happening out there in the world first and then look inside and put the two together in some productive way."

We need to be able to look at both sides of life. We must be able to face the joy and wonder of life as well as the pain, injustice and absurdity of it.

He calls this the dark side of life or the "left hand of God". A beautiful phrase. Most of us are quite content to be at the right hand of God. But none of us wants to suffer the passion of sitting at the left hand of God. We don't want to suffer rejection.

"My recent encounter with cancer is a good example. I had been preaching about the painful mystery of things for many months and then it reached and grabbed me and got my attention.

"That's how it happens. You're going along fine, things are going well and then wham, you're struck with the left hand of God. You see the terrible pain and injustice and absurdity that's part of everything, either in your own life or the lives of those around you.

"Then if you are open you are driven back to the inner place so that you can try to make sense of it all somehow. And of course no one can make sense out of it. One just learns to live with it gracefully."

Only those who have spent time in some sort of hellish pain will recognise the beauty in those words.

Getting in touch with feelings is essential for growth. But Rohr has a word of warning.

"God knows, we men need to get in touch with feelings in this society and thank God many are making the effort. But what are you going to do with those feelings? Where are those feelings going to lead you? You have to do something in the real world, not just indulge or feel your feelings all day long."

In the real world there is injustice. It has to be fought.

"I feel that the poverty, injustice and absurdity that we see when we look around us mirrors our own inner poverty, injustice and absurdity. The poor man or woman outside is an invitation to the poor man or woman inside."

As you learn compassion and sympathy for the brokenness of things, then you learn compassion and sympathy for the brokenness within yourself. You realise that you're a poor person too.

And what about the struggle to be holy in today's world?

Conversion means self surrender, letting go of control and trusting. That's difficult for us. You can't set out to surrender. If you take it on as a project then it becomes an ego adventure and leads nowhere. Then you're back in control again in the name of being surrendered to God's will. Surrender is a tricky business. It's not something you do. It's something which is done to you.

"You can't tell a 20-year-old kid about surrender. If you do he will turn it into a glorification of self." And, says Rohr, that's what's happening to many young idealistic seminarians and religious in our Church.

"There comes a point, usually about the mid-30s or early 40s, when you realise that you've got to start letting go. That you're trying to control reality in life too much.

"So you end up pushing people around and manipulating events and pretty soon God is no longer in charge. You are in charge, every step of the way, making sure you feel the feelings you want to feel and never have to face any discomfort or pain that you don't want to face. Some people never grow out of that.

"We're too much in the grip of an institutional definition of holiness. I was told, as a young man, about St. Aloysius, who always kept his head down whenever he was confronted by a beautiful woman.

"That's not holiness, that's weird. Why should God create the beautiful form and then ask us not to look at it. It doesn't mean I have to possess it or lust after it, but I can surely enjoy it and let it be."

Where have you heard that before, I ask in all modesty?

"The church, too often, has defined holiness as subservience and obedience because that's the kind of person those in power want around them so that they can stay in power."

He makes a wonderful plea for tolerance. Both the old and the new churches are lacking in it.

"On the one hand, we can't be naive about evil. We have to name it when we see it, in ourselves and in others. But we must not immediately damn the other side as totally without merit or conscience.

"All of us are looking for the moral high ground. I see people doing it with diets, with the environment and the social issues. We hate the old church for being so dogmatic and so authoritarian, but woe to you if you are caught eating a piece of red meat or not recycling an aluminium can. These actions can now be considered as sinful as fornication was a generation ago.

"We have to love our churches. On the one hand, the church is a glorious face of Christ. On the other it's the whore of Babylon, totally unfaithful to Christ. It pretends to be absolutely certain about birth control or marriage or women priests (about which Christ said nothing) yet it has comfortable doubts about violence, about riches and about wealth (about which Christ was absolutely clear)."

He has faith in the young too.

"It has taken me 48 years to begin to come to some kind of honest and real appreciation of the spiritual world. What chance has an 18-year-old bewildered kid?

"Faith is giving away what you do not yet have. That's why it's faith. It operates partly out of complete blindness.

"Nowadays, faith has come to mean holding on to answers, finding certitude, having clarity about things, being sure we're absolutely right before we move on or take a risk.

"But a look at our tradition will show that faith is really the opposite of certitude. Rather it is being willing to move into darkness, into not being sure.

"It means taking risks, allowing ourselves to be taken advantage of, having the grace to move through chancy, uncertain waters, letting go of control and trusting that God will always be there. It means living with the mystery of things, not knowing for sure what's going to happen or that it will turn out okay."

As he looks back on his life now, facing death from cancer has taught him a simple lesson. That when he prayed: "Help me now, and at the hour of my death," he didn't expect that his prayer would help him to do it.

He looks back on his life and sees the two hands of God at work. The right hand of God carried him through the good times and the left hand of God taught him about his brokenness.

"At the time I may not have seen it, but looking back I do."

I know it's tough going. But if you grasp what Rohr says, you're well on the way to a meaningful life. And heavy-handed institutions won't get you down. Try it. It works.

Why I Hated God...And Was Cured By Cancer

Here's an interesting story. It's a story written by Allison, (not her real name). I found it fascinating and I hope you do too. She got cancer, hated God and herself and then discovered that hate may have caused her cancer.

"I'll never forget the day my doctor told me that I had cancer. I don't remember driving home. I locked the doors, closed the curtains and fell to the living room floor, wrapped in an old blanket.

"The first feeling I remember was anger. I was angry at my husband for not being with me, even though I had insisted on going to the doctor alone. I was angry at my doctor for not being more understanding. But most of all, I was angry at God for doing this to me.

"It didn't take long for me to see why God was punishing me. I was bad. I was no good. I deserved it. Even so, I was still mad at God for actually doing it. I screamed at Him: 'I hate You, I hate You. Why are You punishing me like this? Leave me alone'."

Then she was still for a long time. After a while she realised the family would be coming home soon. She had to get busy. She washed her face, put on fresh make-up and started getting the dinner.

"The next few days, as I prepared for surgery, I was confused. When I was alone I was full of anger and rage. I hated God and didn't hesitate to say so. But I hated myself too, for feeling the way I did and for not being able to turn to God for comfort and support when I needed it most.

"In my confusion I did something completely out of character for me. It would have far reaching results. I started writing to a friend. I felt comfortable telling him how I felt, since nobody who knew me lived close to him. He was safe. My letters were full of anger, bitterness and resentment.

"His, on the other hand, were full of compassion and he spoke again and again of God's love for me. But I wasn't having any of that, though eventually I agreed that I would visit him after my operation.

"The day before going to the hospital a friend stopped by and asked if he could pray with me. I told him he could pray if he wanted but I didn't. He prayed Psalm 116. And I heard the words: 'I fell into distress and sorrow, and I called upon the name of the Lord, Oh Lord! Save my life.'

"The words touched me. I fought back the tears. In these words I rediscovered the God I had lost. Instead of hating and punishing me, God was hearing my call. Later, alone in the hospital room, I repeated the prayer. 'Oh Lord, Save my life.'

"The next day I believe God did just that. The cancer had not spread. The doctor was sure I would make a complete recovery. But still I was troubled.

"Why had I been so angry? Why, in particular, had I been angry with God? I was relieved to be cured but questions about myself and my relationship with God lingered.

"A week later I went to visit my friend. As in his letters, he talked of God's love for me. He told me that God does not send illness to punish people.

"That would be as unthinkable as me wishing a serious disease on one of my sons. I listened. He made sense to my mind but my heart wasn't convinced.

"After returning home I decided to pray for ten minutes a day. The quiet time would be good for me and would be healing. But I also wanted to try to understand in my heart what my friend told me about God and God's love for me.

"I decided I would just try to be alone with God in silence.

"At first, clearing my mind was difficult. Soon however, I realised how good I felt after praying. Gradually, my earlier refusal to pray became remote. So did my anger.

"Increasingly I became aware of how out of proportion my anger had been. Did all cancer patients react this way? Why had I?

She began reading books on healing. They talked of human wholeness and the connection between the mind and the body and the pain childhood experiences can cause in later life.

Often, they said, this pain is hidden. Could the reason for her anger be buried in her childhood? Could her anger have caused the cancer?

"At this point, my childhood became the focus of prayer. I asked

God to lead me back through it. I kept a notebook beside me and made notes of the memories that surfaced.

"The first couple of times brought familiar memories — the times my father forced me to lie on my bed while he beat me with my pink hairbrush. But then I started remembering things I had forgotten or buried.

"One day, for instance, while he was beating me with the hairbrush, it broke. That became a kind of pattern. Familiar memories would surface to be followed by other experiences I had forgotten and suppressed.

"In recalling my father beating me I remembered his words which had been long buried too, about how I was a bad child. How I never did anything right. How things that went wrong were all my fault. His message came across clearly to me; I was bad.

"No wonder I thought I deserved the cancer. I remembered too how as a child I ached to be hugged and kept wondering why my parents never held me.

"Like many couples at the time, my parents followed the maxim, children should be seen and not heard. But in their case it applied to emotions as well as words.

"Once as a teenager I slammed a door in anger and was locked in my room to break me of my temper. That was a forgotten memory that surfaced.

"So too did the memory that my mother used to slap me across the face. Yet, all the while I was not allowed to express any kind of anger. No wonder I was so full of it now."

Often her memories focused on how respected her parents were. They were an average middleclass family who took part in church events and everything in the community.

"But in the midst of this correctness I lived in terror. In fact, it was becoming more and more clear as a result of my prayer.

"As the painful memories kept coming, I began offering them to God and asking that they be taken from me. Then I would be silent and seek comfort by just being in God's presence.

"Later I was directed to a psychologist who, luckily for me, was a Christian and encouraged me to continue this form of prayer."

He made Allison dig deeper and deeper into her childhood.

"I wrote about why I never played with dolls as a child of four and I was shocked to discover that it was because I didn't want my parents showing any kind of tenderness.

"Increasingly I turned to God and my psychologist to release my anger. With the psychologist I would imagine my parents sitting opposite me and I would scream at them, 'Why didn't you love me? Why didn't you ever say you loved me? Why wouldn't you ever hold me? You never cared how much you hurt me."

Her most difficult times were with her mother. Their conversations had always been superficial. Now Allison wanted to share deeper conversations with her mother and hope maybe that she could even get an apology from her. Maybe they could just cry in each other's arms. Maybe finally Allison could be held. But none of it was possible.

"I knew if I tried anything like that they would be denying, there would be bitterness and the end of any relationship. So, we continue talking about shopping and eating or anything, and that's the way it is today.

"I was never able to communicate with my father either. He died several years ago. Occasionally I saw hints of sensitivity in him but, as with my mother, we were never able to share feelings.

"When he was dying he tried to talk to me alone but frankly I avoided it. I was afraid of what he might say. Now I'll never know what he wanted to tell me. Was it that he was sorry? Did he want to tell me he loved me? Since his death I have often prayed and found comfort sharing my feelings and as a result I have forgiven him and I feel closer to him since death than I did in life…

"Several years have passed since I lay sobbing on the living room floor. The cancer is gone and has not returned. The anger too is gone, though it occasionally returns, but it does so less often and when it does I can deal with it better.

"Most of my painful childhood memories have surfaced and have been released. I no longer feel I am bad and indeed I know I am not.

"I know in my heart that God didn't punish me but loves me and healed me. Increasingly I am aware of God holding me in His arms, not only when I'm up there in my cloud but while I'm down here on earth trying to make for my children the loving family that I never had as a child myself."

And that's how Allison was actually cured by cancer.

How To Cope With A Marriage Break-Up

Marriage break-up is much in the news. Apart from the fact every family knows it at that first hand now, the papers are full of it.

Di and Charles have their marriage problems on the front page of every paper in the world. Just like Anne and Mark and Andrew and Fergie had.

Princess Caroline of Monaco got an annulment from the Catholic Church, and critics said only the rich and famous get them. The uninformed always say foolish things.

Yet 10 years ago when Prince Charles had a *royal friend* who did not get an annulment, he went on record as saying that the Catholic church seemed to give annulments to everyone except the rich and famous. He hit out at the Church for being so insensitive in this day and age.

Maybe he was angry because he really wanted to marry a Catholic, but his own church forbade him having anything to do with Catholics. And still does.

If he ever gets to the throne, he might well repeal the law which forbids his like from marrying Catholics. A peculiar form of bigotry in this day and age — to use his own phrase.

Enough of this religious in-fighting.

Whether you're Di, Charles, Anne, Mark, Andrew, Fergie, Caroline or an ordinary Joe Soap, marriage break-up is a cruel, humiliating process. It should not be a matter of gossip. It leaves one feeling ugly and a failure.

Grief is ugly. The journey through it is excruciating. You can't go through it without bearing scars.

Break-up, call it any name you wish — separation, annulment or divorce — is a grief, and leaves the scars of death in its wake.

But we have a choice. You can either *go* through a separation or you can *grow* through a separation.

Many people who have come through it are more realistic, more compassionate, more human — for having travelled the road of grief.

Live through a separation and eventually the painful wounds will heal. The secret is to choose *life,* not death.

From my own observations, and with the help of people who have been down the road, here are 10 helpful hints.

1. Live in the real world.

When you've loved somebody deeply it is difficult to part. There are so many hurts, so many reminders. Every song on the radio, people walking hand in hand, TV commercials, films — all remind you of the way it used to be. They make you angry that it is no longer so.

Sooner rather than later, you must realise that the separation really is happening to you. You have to face the shock.

Many prolong the agony by clinging to false hopes that they and their spouse will get back together again. Many can't accept that some stories do not have a happy ending.

Look realistically at your situation. Be honest with yourself. For grief to heal you must take responsibility for your life as it is now. Accept reality.

2. Don't rush grief.

If your marriage or relationship has broken up, there's a mourning period similar to the loss of a partner through death. Regardless of the circumstances of the breakdown of your relationship — who started it, how inevitable it was — you have lost something important in your life. And you need time to grieve. Denying or suppressing your feelings or sorrow only prolongs the agony.

This is not the same as wallowing in useless mourning. Useless mourning is surrounding yourself in self-pity or blame, or guilt. Pretending to yourself that everything was either your fault or someone else's.

Be careful too of the friends you have. Many of them feed into this mocking self-pity. If it's not handled properly it will lead to a deep depression. And that's worse than the pain of break-up or the grief.

3. Live your new life.

No matter what happens it will take time to adjust to your new life. There can be some practical difficulties, i.e., moving house, finding new employment, living on the breadline, making arrangements to collect the children, taking on additional household responsibilities yourself.

So, give yourself all the time you need to get used to the adjustments. Don't be rushed by others. Take it at your own speed — as long as you ensure there is some motion in the emotions.

Give yourself time to plan.

A good idea is to list your fears. When you see them in print you can deal with them more easily.

If your finances are tight, do some book-keeping with your income and expenses. And tackle your plans, one step at a time.

Be careful not to try to solve all your problems by running headlong into a new relationship. As Hemingway said: "Life breaks us all sometimes, but some grow strong at broken places." Make sure you give yourself time to heal and be strong at the broken places.

4. Learn to pray.

It's probably the last thing you want to do. But you do need to find the formula to let your anger out. Anger with your spouse or partner. Anger with God. Deal with it in prayer rather than by praying words.

For a time you will need to allow yourself the "why me?" bit. But don't sit forever in the "why me" corner. A much better question is: "How can I move forward from where I am now?"

You'll need someone to help you through the bitterness. There is always the revenge factor. You want to take every penny you can from your spouse. Or you'll want to bargain over children. It's a horrible thing to do but most couples do it, and it only delays the recovery process.

A break up can be a battleground but it need not be a never-ending battleground.

Religion can help you through the bitterness. You'll need time to be angry at the church too. The self-righteousness of some of its members will alienate you. But don't let the illegitimates get you down.

If you feel you cannot have another relationship and remain in the Church, you will be extremely angry. Don't deny it yet. A compassionate priest or minister can often help to restore your faith, not only in the church but in God as well.

5. Remember your friends.

They will listen to you if they are true friends, without taking sides or giving advice. Friends like that are a godsend.

The biggest difficulty will be with those people who are friendly with both you and your former spouse. Allow them to be that. Don't be angry that they haven't taken your side. Misery doesn't have to grow.

Make new friends. It is important to get to know happy, healthy people who don't remind you of your past. They will help you to allow the past to die and to live and grow in the present.

6. You may need professional counselling.

If you do, don't be ashamed: go and get it. Any good counsellor will help you to see yourself in a new light and will enable you to find strength to cope with the situation.

Remember that counsellors can *help* you through it. They cannot *go* through a separation for you. It's essentially a do-it-yourself process.

7. Be balanced.

When you're in the middle of a trauma it's difficult to keep your whole life from going out of balance. Just because your emotions are in a heap doesn't mean that you have to allow your body to become fat and slobby too. Take exercise. It will help your appetite, improve your sleep, and eventually, will pull your emotions into balance as well.

8. Mind the child.

Keeping contact with your former spouse can be difficult. But if you have children it is necessary.

The problem with a separation or divorce is that it really is a death but it's an incomplete death.

It may be a painful experience but a session is needed whereby you work out the details of custody, visiting, and discipline.

Never criticise your spouse in front of the children.

9. Communicate openly with your children.

Tell them that they are not to blame. Just because you are separating from or divorcing your spouse doesn't mean that your children have to be separated from them too.

Reassure them that you're not separating from *them* either. This is particularly true of smaller children but we sometimes forget that a breakup can be devastating on growing children too.

10. Time heals.

Healing will take its own time. There is no magic cure. Give yourself as much time as you need to come to a peaceful resolution. A separation is not an event, but a process. It's the first step to recovery. You can only go through the process one minute, one hour and, if you're lucky, one day, at a time.

Stop blaming yourself. Not every relationship works. You're not a failure. As long as you continue to choose *life*, not death, you are doing what God wants. Once you decide where real life, true life, is, your duty is to make that choice. To settle for death is the ultimate failure.

Today

There are two days in every week about which we should not worry, two days which should be kept free from fear and apprehension.

One of these days is *yesterday* with its mistakes and cares, its faults and blunders, its aches and pains. Yesterday has passed forever beyond our control.

All the money in the world cannot bring back *yesterday*. We cannot undo a single act we performed; we cannot erase a single word we said. Yesterday is gone.

The other day we should not worry about is *tomorrow* with its possible adversities, its burdens, its large promise and poor performance. Tomorrow is also beyond our immediate control.

Tomorrow's sun will rise, either in splendour or behind a mask of clouds — but it will rise. Until it does, we have no stake in tomorrow, for it is yet unborn.

This leaves only one day — today. Any man can fight the battles of just one day. It is only when you and I add the burdens of those two awful eternities — yesterday and tomorrow — that we break down.

It is not the experience of today that drives men mad — it is remorse or bitterness for something which happened yesterday and the dread of what tomorrow may bring.

A Man Called Peter

This is the story of the ups and downs of the man known as Peter the Rock. It applies to every man, woman, child, lay person, priest — and, especially, bishop.

Looking at Peter's life, he seemed to have it all. He was the first Pope. Jesus called Peter a rock because that's what his name meant and he was so steadfast that Jesus could build his church right there.

Jesus gave him the keys of the Kingdom of Heaven. They say he'll be on guard when we want to get through the pearly gates.

Peter cured a man who was crippled from birth. He brought Dorcas back to life. And he was the man who baptised the first gentile Christian, Cornelius.

According to the Bible, people jockeyed to stand in Peter's shadow, because even that seemed to bring healing.

Peter was imprisoned and beaten many times for his faith and was finally crucified upside down on a cross in Rome. He could have been crucified the proper way up but Peter didn't think he was worthy to die in exactly the same way Jesus did.

When you hear all these achievements there's only one conclusion. We have nothing in common with this great saint. He's a superman. He's strong. He's brave. No wonder Jesus took him to be the leader of the Apostles and the church.

But there's another side to Peter. A shadow side. He wasn't so holy and so perfect after all.

The Gospels make it clear that Peter had as many weaknesses as any of us have. Even after Pentecost he showed his humanity. His choices were flawed.

Once upon a time, Jesus had a rough day. It began badly for him when he heard that his cousin and friend, John the Baptist, had been beheaded. So, naturally he wanted some time to grieve and to think and to pray. He got into a boat and rowed alone to a deserted place.

Unfortunately though, the people saw him leave and they followed him by walking along the shoreline. When Jesus landed at his place of solitude he found a crowd of thousands waiting there, wanting to be healed. They cashed in on his compassion. So, all day he preached and cured.

By evening time there was no food and no place to buy it. So Jesus took what little food there was, five loaves and two fishes, and somehow multiplied it to feed the five thousand men, not to mention the women and children who had been gathered there.

At the end of the day he still wanted time to pray. He sent the apostles to cross the Sea of Galilee in a boat. The night was miserable and they were rowing against heavy wind, making little headway. By four in the morning they had hardly gone more than a mile or two and they were exhausted.

They looked ahead and saw what appeared to be a ghost. Nothing but a ghost would be walking across the top of the water, telling them to "take courage".

Peter jumped up and shouted: "Lord, if it is you, command me to come to you in the water." He got the nod and Peter climbed over the side of the boat and to his amazement began to walk across the top of the water, the same as the master.

By now he realised it wasn't a ghost at all.

But when the winds howled and the sting of the salt spray pelted his face the little inner voice said to Peter: "What do you think you're doing, you can't walk on water, you're going to drown..."

And the moment the thought hit him, he began to sink. The freezing water soaked his clothes and weighed him down even more. In one last throw of the dice he cried out: "Lord, save me:"

Instantly, Jesus was before him stretching out his hand. He pulled Peter to the top of the water. You can imagine how foolish Peter felt when Jesus said to him: "Oh you of little faith, why did you doubt?"

Peter learned a lesson. He asked himself that night why he had doubted. And he came to the conclusion that he had listened to the voices of the world instead of the master's voice. He relied on his own strength, he took his eyes off Jesus. Peter learned a good lesson.

Peter was a man who liked to be thought well of. Once he refused to eat with gentile Christians because he feared that the Jewish Christians would criticise him. That was a bad choice, as he soon learned.

And there's more to the dark side of Peter. He bragged about his achievements and then had to eat his words when he couldn't deliver. He said to Jesus: "Even though I should have to die with you, I will not deny you." But before dawn the next day, Peter repeatedly deserted Jesus and denied that he even knew him.

His advice wasn't always accurate either. When Jesus told his diciples he had to suffer and die, Peter took Jesus aside and began to tell him that He was wrong. Jesus scolded him, saying: "Get behind me, Satan, you're not thinking as God does but as human beings do."

Did you ever turn your back on a friend when you were scared? Peter did: he ran away from Jesus in the garden of Gethsemane.

But despite Peter's weaknesses, Jesus never turned his back on him. The only question he was ever asked by Jesus was: "Do you love me?" And there was never any doubt about that.

There are many lessons Peter can tell us. Jesus understands our weakness. He is willing to forgive us for anything we do, if, like Peter, we are sorry and we say we want to change.

The one thing we ought to have in common with Peter is his answer to the question: "Do you love me?"

On The Side of The Angels

What do you do when you're burdened by guilt and see the starving refugees on the TV, while you sit down to a good meal? Usually, very little.

Which is all very fine except that it will be no good when we try to get into heaven. Cain tried that one. He said he was not his brother's keeper. God surprised him by telling him he was. So, how are we going to keep our brothers?

The first thing we must do is to understand the problems better. Go behind the headlines. In countries where there is oil, the western world will go to any lengths to intervene. In poor countries where there is little to lose, nobody bothers.

It means that we have to be prepared to pay more for petrol so that the poor of that country can have a better life. There is no gain without pain.

Secondly, realise that the underdog is specially loved by Jesus.

Take a look at the friends of Jesus. He was a personal friend — not just an acquaintance — of prostitutes, lepers, (he would be a friend of AIDS victims today), itinerants, — he himself was a traveller.

He chose his followers from the lower class. He challenged the upper class. He didn't like lawyers, priests, politicians. They looked down on the ordinary people. And Jesus didn't like them for it.

And thirdly, it's not just a matter of being on the side of the underdog, it's doing something about it. We must devote time, resources, energies and talents to looking after those who are on the margins of society.

It means ensuring that nobody is discriminated against. Be involved in politics and in the church to make sure your voice is heard. Let those who are illiterate or who cannot speak find their thoughts expressed in your words and your speeches.

Be involved, not in the rather dirty politics of self promotion and shady deals, but in politics of working for the good of the local people and the local community.

Treat all people equally. Here, the churches are the greatest offenders of all. It is indefensible that women are treated unjustly in churches and especially in the Catholic church.

It means realising that charity begins at home. So does justice. Get to know your husband, your wife, your children, before you tell other people what to do.

You can't spend all your time trying to get to know them, because that can often be a waste of time too. But you must make an attempt.

Make your family a model of justice, rather than a dictatorship. This applies especially to churches. Too often our churches are run by small-minded dictators. There's no real partnership with laity, clergy and religious congregations.

In the north of this country, those who are trying to bring about integrated education are absolutely and utterly frustrated by the mainline churches. Some of those church leaders go to great lengths to sit down with paramilitaries. But they will not allow the children in integrated schools to be ministered to.

And so you see, looking at those pictures of the starving babies on television does have implications. By all means, eat your meal and enjoy it. But look around for ways to practise justice in your life, your family, your church, your community.

Women Priests

I was delighted that the Anglican Church voted for the ordination of women. That said, I'm bound to say I'm still not happy with the reasoning used. It seems based on expediency, rather than scripture, and owed more to feminism than theology.

While all arguments add to the picture, scripture and theology are the essential ones.

The Anglicans often discussed sexuality when priesthood was the issue.

I first wrote in favour of women priests 17 years ago. I thought then it was just around the corner for all churches.

Later when I studied the issue more fully, the experts told me they had women priests in the first centuries of Christianity. It was no big deal.

In the meantime I have listened with an open mind to scholars and theologians in many religious traditions arguing the point. Nobody has given me any good reason, apart from practice, why women should not be ordained to the priesthood. And that's where I stand.

I believe it is essential that we take risks for good. We should never confine Christ to our little ways of thinking and acting.

Not ordaining women was, I believe, a sign of the times of back then. Women and men had distinct roles. Priesthood was only one area of division.

Ordaining women is equally a sign of our times, a sign of enlightenment.

A sign that we have damaged the body of Christ by confining him too firmly within historical customs and prejudices.

It is a sign that all people are equal, that gifts are not wrapped in blue or pink, that service is the duty and the privilege of all Christians, not just a few hand-picked males.

It is not a question of changing the priesthood to suit modern times. Rather it is extending the same opportunity of ministering so that women who feel called may do so.

Mind you it won't solve all the problems. Women will bring special gifts.

But they will also fall into the same traps (and a few new ones) as males have done for centuries.

They are part of the human race too, with all the goodness of humans and with all the inexplicable faults.

Take politics, for example. We thought that when women took to politics, we'd have a better society. Unfortunately, women politicians are as good and as awful as their male counterparts.

They have caused as much hatred, made as many mistakes, started as many wars, introduced as much damaging legislation, and have been as unjust in their treatment of the poor.

In short, they have lost their special gifts and have become tougher, harsher people with little compassion and less understanding.

Women priests in all probability will be the same.

Already they have taken the worst aspects of priesthood on board. They dress ridiculously. They preach irrelevant sermons in a put-on voice. They wear short male-like haircuts and larger-than-life Roman collars. Why are they so afraid to be feminine?

You'll gather that I don't see women priests as the saviours of Christianity. I see it as a proper opening up of the gift of priesthood to women.

My fear though, is that in the midst of all the talk about women priests, we are neglecting to examine the most vital question of all: How relevant will the ordained full-time ministry be in 20 years?

Is it not priesthood itself which needs to be overhauled?

In the modern world can we justify "layers" of Christianity?

Would we not be better employed looking at ways of encouraging the wonderful calling of the laity?

It could just be possible that all the talk of women priests is a con, ultimately. And the gifts of the laity will go unrecognised and under used for another 10 years.

That would be a real tragedy. That would be the perfect example of the attitude so soundly lashed by Christ in the pharisees.

Another issue raised by the Anglican decision was schism. The threat that some of the people who cannot accept that decision in the Anglican church will somehow cross back to the Roman Catholic church.

Some people may feel called, as part of their journey of faith, to do so. Which is fine, but if the only reason for crossing is the sex of your priest, you should stay put.

The Catholic church has not yet begun to discuss this question officially, but I suspect that there are at least as many in favour of women priests in the Catholic church as there are in the Anglican church.

And Catholics have quite enough people already who hold onto the wrong traditions for the wrong reasons. We don't need any more people overburdened with prejudice. (If your journey is a matter of principle, that, of course, is an entirely different matter.)

But have you thought of women in the Catholic church who are sick and tired of celibate males telling them what to do, who will feel compelled to cross over to the Anglican church? I suspect many now will.

Their loss will be a terrible blow to our Church.

Finally, it is certain that many ministers will leave the Anglicans and join the Catholic church. That, too, could have an unusual side effect. When one of those ministers and his wife, take over your parish, and become your priest and his wife (as has happened in other countries), you'll get so used to the idea of married priests that all the ridiculous arguments against married priests will disappear.

In summary, we are in danger of having married priests and women priests — but nobody will be interested in them.

We'll have spent so much time on non-essentials, that we will have neglected the most essential calling of all — namely handing on a living faith in a loving, compassionate God to a people in dire need of God's companionship.

Celebrate You

Recently, I came across a little piece which you could call the Creed of those who are badly bruised in life. It was written by a group of alcoholics to help other alcoholics.

You are worth celebrating.
You are worth everything, You are unique.
In the whole world, there is only one you.
There is only one person with your talents.
Your experience, your gift.
No one can take your place.
God created only one you, precious in his sight.
You have immense potential to love, to care, to create, to grow, to sacrifice, if you believe in yourself.
What doesn't matter is your age, or your colour, or whether your parents loved you or not.
Maybe they wanted to but couldn't.
Let that go, it belongs to the past.
You belong to the now.
It doesn't matter what you have been, the wrong you've done, the mistakes you've made, the people you've hurt.
You are forgiven. You are accepted. You're okay.
You are loved in spite of everything.
So love yourself and nourish the seeds within you.
Celebrate you. Begin now. Start anew.
Give yourself a new birth. Today.
You are you, and that is all you need to be.
You cannot deserve this new life.
It is given freely, a gift.
That is the miracle called God who loves you.
So celebrate the miracle and celebrate you!

Teenagers, Be Warned

Here is an interesting letter from a young girl.

"School holidays have just begun. Many young students will be taking up part-time work. There is a danger in this, as you will see from my experience. Perhaps you could send out a warning.

"I have been working part-time after school for four years. I've just finished my Leaving Cert this year.

"My work was mostly in shops. Earlier this year I was working in a shop. I missed one Saturday evening and was promptly let go.

"A few weeks later I got another job in a shop and I got a stern warning from my mother that no matter what I did I was on no account to lose this job, as we need the money.

"Anyway, I worked in the shop until midnight. I went to the shop from school and after work my employer brought me home in his car. I live out in the country. Everything went grand for weeks until one night on the way home my boss told me that he was giving me a raise in pay, as I had worked hard. He then put his hand on my knee and squeezed it.

"I jerked my knee away. He said I was too touchy and that he could always get someone else a bit more pleasant for the shop. I did not answer him.

"One night on the way home he stopped the car under some trees, put his arm around me and I could not move.

"He then put his other hand up under my skirt and started to grope me. I kept asking him to stop but he paid no heed. This went on for about ten minutes. Then he drove me home.

"Another night he stopped the car again and held me tight in the same way. This time he opened my blouse, fondled and sucked my breasts. He put his hand up under my skirt and inside my pants. This went on for nearly half an hour.

"I sat quiet and said nothing. He kept on asking me to get in the back seat and repeating over and over: 'You like it'.

"I was disgusted but at the same time strangely excited. Looking back I think it was more the fear of my mother finding out which saved me from making a terrible mistake. I am ashamed to say that due to his overpowering persistence and my mounting excitement I was sorely tempted.

"I told my best friend and she told me to quit the job as all he wanted was a conquest and then he would fire me. I could be left with a bundle of trouble.

"I phoned my employer and told him I would not be working there anymore. All he said was: 'Who wants you, you f—ing little b—.'

"I told my mother that I had quit the job and she went wild. She would not listen to any excuse and grounded me. No discos, friends or TV. But extra chores.

"We had a blazing row. It was the first time I ever had the courage to stand up to my mother.

"My dad was not interested, only in his work.

"Are such incidents prevalent around the country, or am I just unlucky?

"Do parents realise the pressure teenagers can be put under?

"I'm sorry for being so explicit but you are a priest and I hope you will understand. Others must be warned in time.

Carmel, (Not real name)."

The Prodigal Mother

This was sent to me by a reader with a very proper insight into how things should happen.

"Whenever I read the story of the Prodigal Son," she began, "I can't help wondering where his mother was. There's no mention of her in the Bible. And the story doesn't make complete sense without her.

"I understand about sons who leave home with great plans, who return when their money is gone. It's easy to understand about a father who welcomes them back, especially sons.

"But where was the mother when all this was going on? Was there no womanly influence at all on the home? There mustn't have been, because without her it would explain why the three men had so much trouble communicating.

"I suspect if the mother had been there, she would have waited for the right moment to talk to her husband. She would have smoothed things out. Then she would have said something like 'I'm very worried about Prodigal. He looks restless lately, and to be quite honest, he is very bored with farm work. If we're not careful, that young fellow is going to pack up and leave us. Maybe you should have a talk with him and straighten things out.'

"Another time she would have taken the son aside and told him: 'I know he doesn't show it, but your father really does love you. He's teaching you everything he can so that you'll be able to stand on your own two feet when he's dead. I know there's more exciting things happening in other places in the world and it is natural that you'd want to get out and go to dances and parties, but if you can stick in there, don't leave, and stay close by, things will work out.'

"Then she would probably have slipped him a few pounds that she had been saving to buy a new coat for herself.

"And the other son, the resentful one. The mother would have told him how much she appreciated his good work. She'd have told him how proud both herself and her husband were of him. She would have ensured that he knew he was getting the farm.

"She would have made a fuss over him. He'd have loved it and claimed to have hated it.

"All of that makes sense. There are many reasons to prove that had there been a woman in that house, things would have worked out differently. But there is one puzzle. There must have been a mother somewhere. 'Roast the fatted calf' doesn't sound like bachelor cooking to me."

And I hope you get the point!

Doorway to Sanity

The story is told of a New York city school teacher who decided he needed to see a psychiatrist. Determined to get first class help, he picked one with a fashionable Park Avenue address.

When he entered the beautifully decorated reception room, he found no one in attendance. Then he saw two panelled doors labelled "Men" and "Women". He pushed open the door marked "Men" and found himself in a second room with two doors — one labelled "Introverts" and the other "Extroverts".

He opened the door marked "Introverts" and found himself in a third room with two doors. These were designated, "Those making more than $100,000 a year" and "Those making less than $100,000 a year".

He walked through the "Less than" door and found himself back on Park Avenue.

The Great Light of Easter

In the olden days many people gathered when darkness was falling. They sat together throughout the night waiting for the sun to rise on Easter Sunday morning. The sun rising became a symbol of the great Son of God rising from the dead.

"The people who lived in darkness see a great light." The people who lived in despair now have hope. The people who thought that life had nothing to offer, now see a reason for living.

Mother Teresa tells a story which happened to her in Melbourne. She visited an old man who lived in poverty. His house was dirty. There were layers of dirt all over the place. Cobwebs hung from the ceiling. The windows were covered over. There was no light in the room. He lived in perpetual dirt and darkness.

But worse still was the mental state in which he lived. His mind was dark. He lived in a world of depression. He thought he hadn't a friend or a family in the whole world.

Mother Teresa began by befriending him. And after a while she ventured to clean the room.

He was annoyed because she did it. But she insisted on cleaning it anyway.

As she tidied the room she found an oil lamp under a stack of papers and rags. She dusted it off and cleaned it. There was still some oil in it. The wick was working. And so she lit the lamp.

She couldn't understand why he wouldn't light it himself. He was living in utter darkness with no electricity in his room but with a lamp, working but unused.

She asked him why he hadn't lit his lamp.

"Why should I light the lamp? I've become so used to the dark that I don't need it myself. Nobody else ever visits me so why should I light the lamp."

She thought for a while and then said to him: "If I promise to send one of the sisters to you each day, will you promise to light the lamp?"

"Yes," he said, "if I hear a human voice I will light the lamp."

A sister went to visit him each day and he did light the lamp. Later he wrote a note to Mother Teresa. It read: " The light you lit in my life is still burning."

The new light which came into that man's life wasn't the light from the lamp. It was the light that a human being brought to him. According to Mother Teresa he lived a happy, uncomplicated life from there on.

That's the chance which is given to each of us, the chance to rise to a new way of life.

One of the most beautiful images in the resurrection stories in the Gospel is the picture of Jesus having breakfast with the disciples. He's telling us that this new life is ordinary life. It's food and drink. Like Eucharist.

New life begins in this world. We don't have to wait for heaven to enjoy new life.

But to enjoy that new life we need to roll the stone away. The Gospel makes a point of telling us that the stone which imprisoned Jesus in the tomb was rolled away.

Easter is an invitation for us to roll the stone away from whatever imprisons and entombs us in a dark way of life.

It's also an invitation for us to roll the stone away from other people's lives. To reach out a hand of peace and friendship to those who need it. To spot those who are imprisoned in the graves of grief or despair. Graves of anger and bitterness and resentment. Graves of jealousy.

It's comforting that Jesus still had the wounds on his body after he rose from the dead.

The wounds and the scars which we pick up through life are therefore valuable. They make us the people we are. They become a source of hope for others.

Just as the passion of Jesus becomes, through his Resurrection, a source of hope for anyone who is suffering. The resurrection gives us a new way of looking at things all right.

Once in New York I met a girl who had been born with poor vision. She was practically blind. She told me that she was almost 10 years old before she realised that not everyone bumped into walls or fell down stairs.

Like many people who are blind, all her dreams were about people with no heads because she had never seen a head.

In her late teenage life she became totally blind and very depressed. She recalled that a crucial moment in her life was when she talked about her depression to her mother. And the mother admitted that she always knew there was a risk she would be born blind but the mother was willing to take the risk anyway.

For a while, this horrified the girl, and made her angry. But then she realised that she had enjoyed life reasonably well and from that moment on she decided she was going to enjoy life even more. She still hated being blind but she made the best of it.

Two years ago, when she was in her early 40s, she met a surgeon who was willing to help her. He did an operation which gave her back her sight.

The strange thing was that she had to learn to live all over again. Even though she hated being blind, she had become used to it; she was comfortable being blind. Now that she could see, she had to learn to cope with a whole new world.

And that's the challenge for us too. The scales have been torn away from our eyes. Jesus has given us hope. It's such a wonderful feeling that we scarcely believe it.

We still seem to live as if there is no hope. We seem to be comfortable in a world of despair. There seems to be a feeling that God wants people to be poor, unhappy, deprived.

Easter is a call to look at and to rise to a new way of life. To roll away the stones that entomb us.

It's an invitation to see the daily resurrection in your life.

The joy of a newborn baby.

The goodness of young people.

It's an invitation to see the goodness within yourself.

It's and invitation to look at the world itself with new eyes.

Of course there is evil in the world but evil can never win now. Evil is so rare that it is still news. The sad day will be when goodness is so rare that it becomes front page news.

And that in itself gives us all "A Little Bit of Hope..."